The
Wiersbe
BIBLE STUDY SERIES

The **Wiersbe**
BIBLE STUDY SERIES

LUKE 1—13

Let the

World Know

That Jesus

Cares

David C Cook®

transforming lives together

THE WIERSBE BIBLE STUDY SERIES: LUKE 1—13
Published by David C Cook
4050 Lee Vance Drive
Colorado Springs, CO 80918 U.S.A.

Integrity Music Limited, a Division of David C Cook
Eastbourne, East Sussex BN23 6NT, England

The graphic circle C logo is a registered trademark of David C Cook.

LCCN 2013937017
ISBN 978-0-7814-0848-6
eISBN 978-1-4347-0714-7

The Team: Steve Parolini, Karen Lee-Thorp, Amy Konyndyk,
Nick Lee, Tonya Osterhouse, Karen Athen
Series Cover Design: John Hamilton Design
Cover Photo: iStockphoto.com

Printed in the United States of America
First Edition 2013

3 4 5 6 7 8 9 10 11 12

073118

Contents

Introduction to Luke 1—13 7

How to Use This Study 9

Lesson 1
The Good News (Luke 1—2) 13

Lesson 2
God's Son (Luke 3—4) 31

Lesson 3
The Difference (Luke 5) 47

Lesson 4
All Things New (Luke 6—7) 63

Lesson 5
Faith Lessons (Luke 8) 81

Lesson 6
Ministry with Purpose (Luke 9—10) 99

Lesson 7
Life Lessons (Luke 11) 115

Lesson 8
A Warning (Luke 12—13) 131

Bonus Lesson
Summary and Review 149

Introduction to Luke 1–13

From Weakness ...

"Pity is a depressant," wrote the eccentric philosopher Friedrich Nietzsche. "A man loses power when he pities."

Nietzsche went mad in the year Adolf Hitler was born, but Hitler carried on that philosophy. Hitler despised other people and stood apart from them. He especially despised the weak and the handicapped, and he developed programs for exterminating them.

Robert Payne wrote, "Even on festive occasions he remained singularly alone, the flow of emotion ceasing abruptly when it came in contact with him.... He demanded for himself an immunity from people" (*The Life and Death of Adolf Hitler*, Praeger, 461).

What a contrast to Jesus Christ, the compassionate Son of Man!

... to Strength

In his gospel, Dr. Luke described our Lord as One who mingled with people, including publicans and sinners, and shared the burdens of the afflicted and the weak. Jesus proved conclusively that pity is a sign of strength, not of weakness, and that God's power flows through loving hearts.

Our world is filled with hurting people who need a loving touch and a word of encouragement. Jesus has put His people here to let the world know that He cares.

His command to us is, "Be compassionate!"

—*Warren W. Wiersbe*

How to Use This Study

This study is designed for both individual and small-group use. We've divided it into eight lessons—each references one or more chapters in Warren W. Wiersbe's commentary *Be Compassionate* (second edition, David C Cook, 2010). While reading *Be Compassionate* is not a prerequisite for going through this study, the additional insights and background Wiersbe offers can greatly enhance your study experience.

The Getting Started questions at the beginning of each lesson offer you an opportunity to record your first thoughts and reactions to the study text. This is an important step in the study process as those "first impressions" often include clues about what it is your heart is longing to discover.

The bulk of the study is found in the Going Deeper questions. These dive into the Bible text and, along with helpful excerpts from Wiersbe's commentary, help you examine not only the original context and meaning of the verses but also modern application.

Looking Inward narrows the focus down to your personal story. These intimate questions can be a bit uncomfortable at times, but don't shy away from honesty here. This is where you are asked to stand before the mirror of God's Word and look closely at what you see. It's the place to take a good look at yourself in light of the lesson and search for ways in which you can grow in faith.

Going Forward is the place where you can commit to paper those things you want or need to do in order to better live out the discoveries you made in the Looking Inward section. Don't skip or skim through this. Take the time to really consider what practical steps you might take to move closer to Christ. Then share your thoughts with a trusted friend who can act as an encourager and accountability partner.

Finally, there is a brief Seeking Help section to close the lesson. This is a reminder for you to invite God into your spiritual-growth process. If you choose to write out a prayer in this section, come back to it as you work through the lesson and continue to seek the Holy Spirit's guidance as you discover God's will for your life.

Tips for Small Groups

A small group is a dynamic thing. One week it might seem like a group of close-knit friends. The next it might seem more like a group of uncomfortable strangers. A small-group leader's role is to read these subtle changes and adjust the tone of the discussion accordingly.

Small groups need to be safe places for people to talk openly. It is through shared wrestling with difficult life issues that some of the greatest personal growth is discovered. But in order for the group to feel safe, participants need to know it's okay *not* to share sometimes. Always invite honest disclosure, but never force someone to speak if he or she isn't comfortable doing so. (A savvy leader will follow up later with a group member who isn't comfortable sharing in a group setting to see if a one-on-one discussion is more appropriate.)

Have volunteers take turns reading excerpts from Scripture or from the commentary. The more each person is involved even in the mundane tasks, the more they'll feel comfortable opening up in more meaningful ways.

The leader should watch the clock and keep the discussion moving. Sometimes there may be more Going Deeper questions than your group can cover in your available time. If you've had a fruitful discussion, it's okay to move on without finishing everything. And if you think the group is getting bogged down on a question or has taken off on a tangent, you can simply say, "Let's go on to question 5." Be sure to save at least ten to fifteen minutes for the Going Forward questions.

Finally, soak your group meetings in prayer—before you begin, during as needed, and always at the end of your time together.

The Good News
LUKE 1—2

Before you begin ...
- *Pray for the Holy Spirit to reveal truth and wisdom as you go through this lesson.*
- *Read Luke 1—2. This lesson references chapters 1, "Hear the Good News!," and 2, "The Lord Is Come!,"* in Be Compassionate. *It will be helpful for you to have your Bible and a copy of the commentary available as you work through this lesson.*

Getting Started

From the Commentary

If ever a man wrote a book filled with good news for everybody, Dr. Luke is that man. His key message is, "For the Son of man is come to seek and to save that which was lost" (Luke 19:10). He presents Jesus Christ as the compassionate Son of Man, who came to live among sinners, love them, help them, and die for them.

In this gospel you meet individuals as well as crowds, women and children as well as men, poor people as well as rich people, and sinners along with saints. It's a book with a message for *everybody*, because Luke's emphasis is on the universality of Jesus Christ and His salvation: "good tidings of great joy, which shall be to all people" (Luke 2:10).

—*Be Compassionate*, page 17

1. Why do you think Luke opened his letter with accounts of the two births? What does this say about Luke? Why was this opening important to the early Christians? What does it say to us today? What does Luke's emphasis on the universality of Jesus teach us about his audience? Whom does his message speak to most directly today?

More to Consider: Read the following passages: Colossians 4:14; 2 Timothy 4:11; and verse 24 of Philemon. What do these verses tell us about Luke? Luke also wrote Acts. What do we learn about the man from this book of the Bible? Is it significant that Luke was a physician? Explain.

2. Choose one verse or phrase from Luke 1—2 that stands out to you. This could be something you're intrigued by, something that makes you uncomfortable, something that puzzles you, something that resonates with you, or just something you want to examine further. Write that here.

Going Deeper

From the Commentary

In the sixth month of Elizabeth's pregnancy, Gabriel brought a second birth announcement, this time to a young virgin in Nazareth named Mary. At least there was variety in his assignments: an old man, a young woman; a priest, a descendent of David the king; the temple, a common home; Jerusalem, Nazareth; unbelief, faith.

The people in Judah disdained the Jews in Galilee and claimed they were not "kosher" because of their contacts with the Gentiles there (Matt. 4:15). They especially despised the people from Nazareth (John 1:45–46). But God in His grace chose a girl from Nazareth in Galilee to be the mother of the promised Messiah!

What do we know about Mary? She was a Jewess of the tribe of Judah, a descendant of David, and a virgin (Isa. 7:14). She was engaged to a carpenter in Nazareth named Joseph (Matt. 13:55), and apparently both of them were poor (Lev. 12:8; Luke 2:24). Among the Jews at that time, engagement was almost as binding as marriage and could be broken only by divorce. In fact, the man and the woman were called "husband" and "wife" even before the marriage took place (compare Matt. 1:19 and Luke 2:5). Since Jewish girls married young, it is likely that Mary was a teenager when the angel appeared to her.

—*Be Compassionate*, page 21

3. Why do people tend to go to one of two extremes in how they view Mary? (Extreme veneration or barely acknowledging her.) Why does she deserve honor? How do we know if we're giving her too much honor? Too little?

From the Commentary

Mary knew *what* would happen, but she did not know *how* it would happen. Her question in Luke 1:34 was not an evidence of unbelief (cf. Luke 1:18); rather, it was an expression of faith. She believed the promise, but she did not understand the performance. How could a virgin give birth to a child?

First, Gabriel explained that this would be a miracle, the work of the Holy Spirit of God. Joseph, her betrothed, would not be the father of the child (Matt. 1:18–25), even though Jesus would be legally identified as the son of Joseph (Luke 3:23; 4:22; John 1:45; 6:42). It's possible that some people thought Mary had been unfaithful to Joseph and that Jesus was "born of fornication" (John 8:41). This was a part of the pain that Mary had to bear all her life (Luke 2:35).

Gabriel was careful to point out that the Baby would be a "holy thing" and would not share the sinful human nature of man. Jesus knew no sin (2 Cor. 5:21), He did no sin (1 Peter 2:22), and He had no sin (1 John 3:5). His body was prepared for Him by the Spirit of God (Heb. 10:5) who "overshadowed" Mary. That word is applied to the presence of God in the Holy of Holies in the Jewish tabernacle and temple (Ex. 40:35). Mary's womb became a Holy of Holies for the Son of God!

—*Be Compassionate*, pages 22–23

4. Read Genesis 18:14. How is God's word to Abraham similar to the encouragement He gave Mary? Read Job 42:2, Jeremiah 32:17, and Matthew 19:26. What does it mean to say that nothing is too hard for

God? For example, can God make a square circle? Can He do something that conflicts with His character?

From the Commentary

> Now that Mary knew she was to become a mother, and that her kinswoman Elizabeth would give birth in three months, she wanted to see Elizabeth so they could rejoice together.
>
> As Mary entered the house, Elizabeth heard her greeting, was filled with the Spirit, and was told by the Lord why Mary was there. The one word that filled her lips was "blessed." Note that she did not say that Mary was blessed *above* women but *among* women, and certainly this is true. While we don't want to ascribe to Mary that which only belongs to God, neither do we want to minimize her place in the plan of God.
>
> The thing that Elizabeth emphasized was Mary's *faith*: "Blessed is she that believed" (Luke 1:45). We are saved "by grace … through faith" (Eph. 2:8–9). Because Mary

believed the Word of God, she experienced the power of God.

—*Be Compassionate*, page 24

5. Review Luke 1:46–56. How does this passage express Mary's faith? What did she believe about God? Compare this passage with 1 Samuel 2:1–10. How did Mary echo Hannah? Read 1 Samuel 1. How was Mary's situation like Hannah's? Why is this significant? What does it say about the relationship between the Old Testament and the New?

From the Commentary

God's blessing was resting abundantly on Zacharias and Elizabeth. He sent them a baby boy, just as He promised, and they named him "John" just as God had instructed. The Jews looked on children as a gift from God and a "heritage from the Lord" (Ps. 127:3–5; 128:1–3), and rightly so, for they are. Israel would not follow the practices of their pagan neighbors by aborting or abandoning their children. When you consider that 1.5 million babies are aborted each year in the United States alone, you can see how far we have drifted from the laws of God.

Traditionally, a baby boy would be named after his father or someone else in the family, so the relatives and neighbors were shocked when Elizabeth insisted on the name *John*. Zacharias wrote "His name is John" on a tablet, and that settled it! Immediately God opened the old priest's mouth, and he sang a hymn that gives us four beautiful pictures of what the coming of Jesus Christ to earth really means.

—*Be Compassionate*, pages 26–27

6. How is Jesus described in Zacharias' song (Luke 1:68–79)? What does it mean to call Jesus "a horn of salvation" (v. 69)? What does it mean to call Him "the rising sun" (v. 78)? What picture of Jesus do these images paint for us today?

From the Commentary

"As weak as a baby!" is a common expression that could not be applied to the Baby Jesus in the manger. While He was as weak as any other baby humanly speaking, He was also the center of power as far as heaven was concerned.

Augustus Caesar was ruling, but God was in charge, for He used Caesar's edict to move Mary and Joseph eighty miles from Nazareth to Bethlehem to fulfill His Word. Rome took a census every fourteen years for both military and tax purposes, and each Jewish male had to return to the city of his father to record his name, occupation, property, and family.

When Mary said, "Be it unto me according to thy word" (Luke 1:38), it meant that from then on, her life would be a part of the fulfillment of divine prophecy. God had promised that the Savior would be a human, not an angel (Gen. 3:15; Heb. 2:16), and a Jew, not a Gentile (Gen. 12:1–3; Num. 24:17). He would be from the tribe of Judah (Gen. 49:10), and the family of David (2 Sam. 7:1–17), born of a virgin (Isa. 7:14) in Bethlehem, the city of David (Mic. 5:2).

—*Be Compassionate*, pages 31–32

7. Review Luke 2:1–7. What role did Caesar unknowingly play in the Christmas story? What are other examples where God intervened in history to help shape the narrative toward His purposes? In what ways is history His story?

From the Commentary

How amazed the angels must have been when they saw the Creator born as a creature, the Word coming as a speechless baby.

The first announcement of the Messiah's birth was given by an angel to some anonymous shepherds. Why shepherds? Why not to priests or scribes? By visiting the shepherds, the angel revealed the grace of God toward mankind. Shepherds were really outcasts in Israel. Their work not only made them ceremonially unclean, but it also kept them away from the temple for weeks at a time so that they could not be made clean. God does not call the rich and mighty; He calls the poor and the lowly (Luke 1:51–53; 1 Cor. 1:26–29).

The Messiah came to be both the Good Shepherd (John 10) and the Lamb of God sacrificed for the sins of the world (John 1:29). Perhaps these shepherds were caring for the flocks that would provide sacrifices for the temple services. It was fitting that the good news about God's Shepherd and Lamb be given first to humble shepherds.

Shepherds are not easily fooled. They are practical men of the world who have little to do with fantasy. If they said that they saw angels and went and found the Messiah, then you could believe them. God selected hard-working men to be the first witnesses that His Son had come into the world.

First, one angel appeared (Gabriel?) and gave the glad announcement, and then a chorus of angels joined him and gave an anthem of praise. For the first time in centuries, the glory of God returned to earth. If brave shepherds were afraid at what they saw and heard, then you can be sure it was real!

—*Be Compassionate*, page 33

8. Read 2 Corinthians 8:9. How does this passage speak to what the angels observed with Jesus' birth? (See also 1 Tim. 3:16.) Why is this mysterious and miraculous event so important to our faith? How would Christianity be different today if Jesus' birth had been anything but a miracle?

More to Consider: Read Job 38:7. What does this tell us about the angels' role in God's story for mankind? What do the angels reveal to us about God's glory and the purpose of that glory in God's plan (see John 1:14; Eph. 1:6, 12, 14)?

From the Commentary

> Dr. Luke tells us about three important meetings in the temple in Jerusalem: the child Jesus met Moses (Luke 2:20–24), Simeon (Luke 2:25–35), and Anna (Luke 2:36–38).
>
> Moses (vv. 21–24). Note that the word *law* is used five times in Luke 2:21–40. Though He came to deliver His people from the bondage of the law, Jesus was "made under the law" and obeyed its commands (Gal. 4:1–7). He did not come to destroy the law but to fulfill it (Matt. 5:17–18).
>
> Simeon (vv. 25–35). Simeon and Anna, like Zacharias and Elizabeth, were a part of the faithful Jewish remnant that eagerly looked for their Messiah (Mal. 3:16).
>
> Anna (vv. 36–38). Her name means "grace," and she was a godly widow of great age. There are forty-three references to women in Luke's gospel, and of the twelve widows mentioned in the Bible, Luke has three (Luke 2:36–40; 7:11–15; 21:1–4; and note 18:1–8). It isn't difficult to see the heart of a physician in Luke's presentation.
>
> —*Be Compassionate*, pages 35–39

9. Review Luke 2:21–38. How would you put Simeon's response to meeting Jesus in your own words? Why was it significant that Anna is mentioned? How were widows typically treated during this time in

history and in this culture? (See Ex. 22:21–22; Deut. 10:17–18; 14:29; Isa. 1:17; see also 1 Tim. 5:3–16.)

From the Commentary

Having obeyed the law in everything, Mary and Joseph returned to Nazareth, which would be our Lord's home until He started His official ministry. There were many Jewish men with the name *Jesus* (Joshua), so He would be known as "Jesus of Nazareth" (Acts 2:22), and His followers would be called "Nazarenes" (Acts 24:5; see Matt. 2:23). His enemies used the name scornfully and Pilate even hung it on the cross (Matt. 21:11), but Jesus was not ashamed to use it when He spoke from heaven (Acts 22:8). That which men scorned (John 1:46), Jesus Christ took to heaven and made glorious!

What did Jesus do during the "hidden years" at Nazareth? Dr. Luke reports that the lad developed physically, mentally, socially, and spiritually (Luke 2:40, 52). In His incarnation, the Son of God set aside the independent use of His own divine attributes and submitted Himself wholly to the Father (Phil. 2:1–11). There are deep mysteries here that no one can fully understand or explain, but we have no problem accepting them by faith.

Jesus did not perform any miracles as a boy, traditions notwithstanding, because the turning of water into wine was the beginning of His miracles (John 2:1–11). He worked with Joseph in the carpenter shop (Matt. 13:55; Mark 6:3) and apparently ran the business after Joseph died. Joseph and Mary had other children during those years (Matt. 13:55–56; John 7:1–10), for the "until" of Matthew 1:25 indicates that the couple eventually had normal marital relations.

—Be Compassionate, page 40

10. Why do we not have much history of Jesus between His birth and the start of His ministry (apart from one incident when He was a young boy)? Would knowing more about Jesus from this time period be a good thing? Why or why not? What does this lack of historical information tell us about God? About His salvation plan?

Looking Inward

Take a moment to reflect on all that you've explored thus far in this study of Luke 1—2. Review your notes and answers and think about how each of these things matters in your life today.

Tips for Small Groups: To get the most out of this section, form pairs or trios and have group members take turns answering these questions. Be honest and as open as you can in this discussion, but most of all, be encouraging and supportive of others. Be sensitive to those who are going through particularly difficult times and don't press for people to speak if they're uncomfortable doing so.

11. What do you think of when you hear the phrase "good news"? What are some ways that this first part of Luke's gospel speaks to you personally? Which of the characters in these chapters would you most like to resemble? What qualities of that person would you like to have?

12. What is your perspective on Mary's role in God's plan? For what qualities does she deserve honor? Do you give her enough honor? Too much? What's the proper place for Mary in your faith story?

13. Caesar played a role in the Christmas story without knowing it. Have you ever witnessed God's hand shaping His plan by using nonbelievers? Explain. How does this affect the way you view your relationships with both believers and nonbelievers?

Going Forward

14. Think of one or two things that you have learned that you'd like to work on in the coming week. Remember that this is all about quality, not quantity. It's better to work on one specific area of life and do it well than to work on many and do poorly (or to be so overwhelmed that you simply don't try).

Do you want to explore the proper place for Mary in your faith story? Be specific. Go back through Luke 1—2 and put a star next to the phrase or verse that is most encouraging to you. Consider memorizing this verse.

Real-Life Application Ideas: Luke's opening chapters are all about joy. The joy of God's Son, the joy of a hopeful future. This week, be intentional about looking for pockets of joy in your life. Make a joy journal to record those things that bring you true joy. Also, look for ways to bring joy to those around you—family members, friends, even coworkers. At the end of the week, take a moment to reflect on how this focus on joy impacted your attitude and your testimony. Then don't stop at one week—look for joy always!

Seeking Help

15. Write a prayer below (or simply pray one in silence), inviting God to work on your mind and heart in those areas you've noted in the Going Forward section. Be honest about your desires and fears.

Notes for Small Groups:

- *Look for ways to put into practice the things you wrote in the Going Forward section above. Talk with other group members about your ideas and commit to being accountable to one another.*

- *During the coming week, ask the Holy Spirit to continue to reveal truth to you from what you've read and studied.*

- *Before you start the next lesson, read Luke 3—4. For more in-depth lesson preparation, read chapter 3, "This Is the Son of God!," in* Be Compassionate.

God's Son
Luke 3—4

Before you begin …
- *Pray for the Holy Spirit to reveal truth and wisdom as you go through this lesson.*
- *Read Luke 3—4. This lesson references chapter 3 in* Be Compassionate. *It will be helpful for you to have your Bible and a copy of the commentary available as you work through this lesson.*

Getting Started

From the Commentary

When John the Baptist appeared on the scene (3:1–2), no prophetic voice had been heard in Israel for four hundred years. His coming was a part of God's perfect timing, for everything that relates to God's Son is always on schedule (Gal. 4:4; John 2:4; 13:1). The fifteenth year of Tiberius Caesar was AD 28–29.

Luke named seven different men in Luke 3:1–2, including a Roman emperor, a governor, three tetrarchs (rulers over a fourth part of an area), and two Jewish high priests. But God's Word was not sent to any of them! Instead, the message of God came to John the Baptist, a humble Jewish prophet.

—*Be Compassionate*, page 45

1. Why did God send His message through John the Baptist? Why choose a humble prophet instead of a well-placed spiritual or political leader? How does the choice of John hint at God's plan for Jesus' ministry?

More to Consider: Why did John the Baptist come resembling Elijah in manner and dress? (See Luke 1:17; Matt. 3:4; 2 Kings 1:8.) What symbolic role does the Jordan River play in this story? (Remember that Israel crossed the Jordan to enter the Promised Land.)

2. Choose one verse or phrase from Luke 3—4 that stands out to you. This could be something you're intrigued by, something that makes you

uncomfortable, something that puzzles you, something that resonates with you, or just something you want to examine further. Write that here.

Going Deeper

From the Commentary

> Keep in mind that John did much more than preach against sin; he also proclaimed the gospel. The word *preached* in Luke 3:18 gives us the English word *evangelize* ("to preach the good news"). John introduced Jesus as the Lamb of God (John 1:29) and told people to trust in Him. John was only the best man at the wedding: Jesus was the Bridegroom (John 3:25–30). John rejoiced at the opportunity of introducing people to the Savior, and then getting out of the way.

> A unique feature about John's ministry was baptism (Luke 20:1–8; John 1:25–28). Baptism was nothing new to the people, for the Jews baptized Gentile proselytes. But John baptized *Jews,* and this was unusual. Acts 19:1–5 explains that John's baptism *looked forward* to the coming of the Messiah, while Christian baptism *looks back* to the finished work of Christ.

But there was something even beyond John's baptism, and that was the baptism that the Messiah would administer (Luke 3:16). He would baptize believers with the Holy Spirit, and this began at Pentecost (Acts 1:5; 2:1ff.). Today, the moment a sinner trusts Christ, he or she is baptized by the Spirit into the body of Christ (1 Cor. 12:13).

—*Be Compassionate*, page 46

3. Why would washing with water have been a fitting symbol of repentance? Why was it an appropriate preparation for the coming of the Messiah? How would Jesus' baptism differ from John's? What is the "baptism of fire" (Luke 3:16–17) that was yet to come?

From the Commentary

The illustrations used in 3:4–20 help us understand the ministry God gave to John.

To begin with, John the Baptist was *a voice* "crying in the wilderness" (Luke 3:4; see also Isa. 40:1–5, John 1:23). He was like the herald who went before the royal procession to make sure the roads were ready for the king. Spiritually speaking, the nation of Israel was living in a "wilderness" of unbelief, and the roads to spiritual reality were twisted and in disrepair. The corruption of the priesthood (instead of one, there were *two* high priests!) and the legalistic hypocrisy of the scribes and Pharisees had weakened the nation spiritually. The people desperately needed to hear a voice from God, and John was that faithful voice.

—Be Compassionate, page 47

4. What was John's primary task? (See Luke 1:16–17, 76–77; John 1:6–8, 15–34.) Why was this task given to a man rather than to angels? How would you describe John as a person, and the way he went about fulfilling his task? Why was that necessary?

From Today's World

There are a lot of voices crying in the wilderness of the Internet today. Everyone who has access to a computer has access to a platform to speak their mind about what they think is important. Facebook, Twitter, Tumblr, and blogs give the common person a forum to spout truth, or lies that purport to be truth, and many are using their platforms to shout for repentance. But with so many voices shouting at the same time, it's hard for people to know whom to listen to. Sometimes the familiar voices of renowned speakers and writers rise to the surface, but at other times, new voices grab the attention of seekers and believers in crisis.

5. How do we know whom to listen to today when it comes to matters of the faith? Is it a positive or negative development that nearly anyone can shout his or her version of the truth? What are our best resources for vetting the claims made by previously unknown men and women? How do we know we're listening to a true prophet of God and not a person simply claiming to be a prophet?

From the Commentary

> One day, after all the others had been baptized, Jesus presented Himself for baptism at the Jordan, and John at first refused to comply (Matt. 3:13–15). He knew that Jesus of Nazareth was the perfect Son of God who had no need to repent of sin. Why then was the sinless Son of God baptized?
>
> —*Be Compassionate*, page 48

6. Review Luke 3:21–38. Why was Jesus baptized? What did His baptism signify? (See Acts 1:21–22; 10:37–38.) What does Jesus tell us in Matthew 3:15 about the reason for His baptism? What did He mean?

From the Commentary

When our Lord came up from the water, the Father spoke from heaven and identified Him as the beloved Son of God, and the Spirit visibly came upon Jesus in the form of a dove (Luke 3:22). Those who deny the Trinity have a difficult time explaining this event.

This is the first of three recorded occasions when the Father spoke from heaven. The second was when Jesus was transfigured (Luke 9:28–36), and the third was during His last week before the cross (John 12:28).

Only Luke mentions that Jesus was praying, and this was only one of many occasions (Luke 5:16; 6:12; 9:18, 28–29; 11:1; 23:34, 46).

Luke interrupted his narrative at this point to give us a genealogy of Jesus. Matthew's genealogy (Matt. 1:1–17) begins with Abraham and moves forward to Jesus, while

Luke's begins with Jesus and moves backward to Adam. Matthew gives us the genealogy of Joseph, the legal foster-father of Jesus, while Luke gives us the genealogy of His mother, Mary. Luke 3:23 can be translated: "When He began His ministry, Jesus was about thirty years old (being supposedly the son of Joseph), the son of Heli [an ancestor of Mary]." Mary herself would not be mentioned because it was unusual for women to be named in the official genealogies, though Matthew names four of them (Matt. 1:3, 5, 16).

—*Be Compassionate*, pages 49–50

7. Luke made a point of noting over and over that Jesus was praying. How is this significant? What does this tell us about Luke's gospel? About how he saw Jesus? Why did Luke include a genealogy? How was this relevant to his audience? Why is it relevant still today?

From the Commentary

Even the enemy must admit that Jesus is the Son of God. "If thou be the Son of God" (Luke 4:3, 9) is not a supposition but an affirmation. It means "in view of the fact that You are the Son of God" (WUEST). Indeed, the fact of His deity was the basis for the first of the three temptations. "Since you are the Son of God," Satan argued, "why be hungry? You can change stones into bread!" Satan wanted Jesus to disobey the Father's will by using His divine power for His own purposes.

Why was Jesus tempted? For one thing, it was proof that the Father's approval was deserved (Luke 4:22). Jesus is indeed the "beloved Son" who always does whatever pleases His Father (John 8:29).

—*Be Compassionate*, page 50

8. What were the different ways Satan tempted Jesus? Why these particular temptations? What do they reveal about Jesus? About Satan's attacks? How are these temptations still challenges for Christians today?

More to Consider: We have at our disposal the same spiritual resources that Jesus used when He faced and defeated Satan: prayer (Luke 3:21–22), the Father's love (v. 22), the power of the Spirit (4:1), and the Word of God ("It is written"). We also have in heaven the interceding Savior who has defeated the Enemy completely. How can we use these resources on a daily basis? Why is it important to be constantly aware of all we have access to? In what ways does Satan use temptation to defeat us? Read James 1:1–8, 13–17. How can God use temptation to bring us closer to Him?

From the Commentary

The events recorded in John 1:19—4:45 took place at the same time as those in Luke 4:14–30, but Matthew, Mark, and Luke did not record them. They moved right into the Lord's ministry in Galilee, and Luke alone reports His visit to His hometown of Nazareth. By now, the news had spread widely about the miracle worker from Nazareth, so His family, friends, and neighbors were anxious to see and hear Him.

A typical synagogue service opened with an invocation for God's blessing and then the recitation of the traditional Hebrew confession of faith (Deut. 6:4–9; 11:13–21). This was followed by prayer and the prescribed readings from the law and from the prophets, with the reader paraphrasing the Hebrew Scriptures in Aramaic.

This was followed by a brief sermon given by one of the men of the congregation or perhaps by a visiting rabbi (see

Acts 13:14–16). If a priest was present, the service closed with a benediction. Otherwise, one of the laymen prayed and the meeting was dismissed.

Jesus was asked to read the Scripture text and to give the sermon.

—*Be Compassionate*, page 54

9. Why was it important to Luke to report this event of Jesus attending public worship? What message does that give churchgoers today? What did Jesus mean when He said that the passage in Isaiah was fulfilled? What does the passage tell us about Jesus' mission?

From the Commentary

Jesus left Nazareth and set up His headquarters in Capernaum (Matt. 4:13–16), the home of Peter, Andrew, James, and John. He taught regularly in the synagogue and astonished the people by the authority of His message (see Matt. 7:28–29). He further astonished them by His authority over the demons.

After the service, Jesus went to Peter's house, and there He healed Peter's mother-in-law. (Dr. Luke noted that she had a "great fever.") At sundown, when the Sabbath had ended and healing was permissible, a host of people brought their sick and afflicted to Peter's house and asked Jesus to help them. Again, He silenced the demons who confessed Him to be the Son of God.

—*Be Compassionate*, page 56

10. Review Luke 4:31–44. Why would a demonized man attend the synagogue? Why did Jesus tell the demons to be still? After a demanding day, Jesus was up early to pray (see Mark 1:35). Why was this so important for Him? Why is it important for us?

Looking Inward

Take a moment to reflect on all that you've explored thus far in this study of Luke 3—4. Review your notes and answers and think about how each of these things matters in your life today.

Tips for Small Groups: To get the most out of this section, form pairs or trios and have group members take turns answering these questions. Be honest and as open as you can in this discussion, but most of all, be encouraging and supportive of others. Be sensitive to those who are going through particularly difficult times and don't press for people to speak if they're uncomfortable doing so.

11. Have you ever met someone who claimed to be a prophet? If so, what was that experience like? Did you believe him or her? Why or why not?

12. Have you been baptized? If so, describe that experience. What did it mean to you? To others? How does John's baptism of Jesus relate to your own baptism?

13. Jesus attended worship, even though He could have chosen to avoid it because it was corrupt. Instead, He went and participated. Have you ever been tempted to avoid church because it's flawed? What are the complaints that tempt you to stay home? Why attend if things aren't going well at church?

Going Forward

14. Think of one or two things that you have learned that you'd like to work on in the coming week. Remember that this is all about quality, not quantity. It's better to work on one specific area of life and do it well than to work on many and do poorly (or to be so overwhelmed that you simply don't try).

If you haven't been baptized, do you want to consider it? Be specific. Go back through Luke 3—4 and put a star next to the phrase or verse that is most encouraging to you. Consider memorizing this verse.

Real-Life Application Ideas: Spend this week contemplating the meaning of baptism. If you've been baptized, review that experience and think about what it meant to you then, and what it means to you now. If you haven't, talk with a pastor or small-group leader about the possibility of being baptized. Then consider what this means in practical terms. How can you honor the symbolism of your baptism in everyday life?

Seeking Help

15. Write a prayer below (or simply pray one in silence), inviting God to work on your mind and heart in those areas you've noted in the Going Forward section. Be honest about your desires and fears.

Notes for Small Groups:

- *Look for ways to put into practice the things you wrote in the Going Forward section. Talk with other group members about your ideas and commit to being accountable to one another.*

- *During the coming week, ask the Holy Spirit to continue to reveal truth to you from what you've read and studied.*

- *Before you start the next lesson, read Luke 5. For more in-depth lesson preparation, read chapter 4, "The Difference Jesus Makes," in* Be Compassionate.

The Difference
LUKE 5

Before you begin …
- *Pray for the Holy Spirit to reveal truth and wisdom as you go through this lesson.*
- *Read Luke 5. This lesson references chapter 4 in* Be Compassionate. *It will be helpful for you to have your Bible and a copy of the commentary available as you work through this lesson.*

Getting Started

From the Commentary

The event in 5:1–11 is not parallel to the one described in Matthew 4:18–22 and Mark 1:16–20. In those accounts, Peter and Andrew were busy fishing, but in this account they had fished all night and caught nothing and were washing their nets. (If nets are not washed and stretched out to dry, they rot and break.) Jesus had enlisted Peter, Andrew, James, and John earlier, and they had traveled with Him in Capernaum and Galilee (Mark 1:21–39), but then they went back to their trade. Now He would call them to a life of full-time discipleship.

It is possible that at least seven of the disciples were fishermen (John 21:1–3).

—*Be Compassionate*, page 59

1. Compare Luke 5:1–11 with Mark 1:16–20. What impression of these men and their calling do you get from Luke? From Mark? What impression do you get of Jesus from each story? What qualities did fishermen have that might have prepared them for a life of ministry?

2. Choose one verse or phrase from Luke 5 that stands out to you. This could be something you're intrigued by, something that makes you uncomfortable, something that puzzles you, something that resonates with you, or just something you want to examine further. Write that here.

Going Deeper

From the Commentary

> If I had fished all night and caught nothing, I would prob-
> ably be *selling* my nets, not washing them to get ready to
> go out again! But true fishermen don't quit. Peter kept
> on working while Jesus used his ship as a platform from
> which to address the huge crowd on the shore. "Every
> pulpit is a fishing boat," said Dr. J. Vernon McGee, "a
> place to give out the Word of God and attempt to catch
> fish."
>
> But there was another side to this request: Peter was a
> "captive audience" as he sat in the ship listening to the
> Word of God. "So then faith comes by hearing, and hear-
> ing by the word of God" (Rom. 10:17 NKJV). In a short
> time, Peter would have to exercise faith, and Jesus was
> preparing him. First He said, "Thrust out a little," and
> then, when Peter was ready, He commanded, "Launch
> out into the deep." If Peter had not obeyed the first
> seemingly insignificant command, he would never have
> participated in a miracle.
>
> —*Be Compassionate*, page 60

3. Why might a "don't quit" attitude have been important for Jesus'
disciples? What kinds of obstacles did they face? How did Jesus take Peter
yard by yard into deeper water in this story? How does He do that with
followers today?

More to Consider: What might Peter's response have been when Jesus took command of the ship and its crew? (Keep in mind that Jesus was a carpenter by trade. See Mark 6:3.) It was a well-known fact that in the Sea of Galilee, you caught fish at night in the shallow water, not in the daytime in the deep water. Knowing this, Peter still obeyed (Luke 5:5). Why?

From the Commentary

Luke 5:12–16 tells of a man who *needed to be changed,* for he was a leper. Among the Jews, several skin diseases were classified as leprosy, including our modern Hansen's disease. In spite of modern medical advances, an estimated ten million people around the world have leprosy. One form of leprosy attacks the nerves so that the victim cannot feel pain. Infection easily sets in, and this leads to degeneration of the tissues. The limb becomes deformed and eventually falls off.

It was the task of the Jewish priest to examine people to determine whether they were lepers (Lev. 13). Infected people were isolated and could not return to normal society until declared "cleansed." Leprosy was used by Isaiah as a picture of sin (Isa. 1:4–6), and the detailed instructions in Leviticus 13—14 would suggest that more was involved in the procedure than maintaining public health.

—*Be Compassionate,* page 61

4. How is sin like leprosy? (See Lev. 13:3, 7–8, 44–46; Jer. 6:14.) People with leprosy were looked on as "stillborn" (Num. 12:12), and garments infected with leprosy were fit only for the fire (Lev. 13:52). How would this healing story have been viewed by the religious leaders of the day? How does this story reveal God's power over sin?

From Today's World

Leprosy has just about been greatly reduced in the modern world, but there are plenty of other diseases that continue to plague mankind. While none of those carries the same weighty emotional and sociological baggage that leprosy did in Jesus' day, that doesn't stop people from associating certain diseases with sinful behaviors. AIDS is the most obvious example of this, of course, but it happens with more common afflictions, too. We continue to judge others—whether aloud or in secret—based on the circumstances they find themselves in, whether those circumstances are of their own making or completely out of their control.

5. Jesus was making a very powerful statement with His healing of lepers. What are the broader implications of that healing? What does Jesus' healing teach us today about the way we ought to approach those whom we consider "unclean" for whatever reason? How can we show love to those who feel marginalized because of sickness or any other factors?

From the Commentary

> By the grace and power of God, this man *was changed!* In
> fact, Jesus even touched the man, which meant that He
> became unclean Himself. This is a beautiful picture of
> what Jesus has done for lost sinners: He became sin for us
> that we might be made clean (2 Cor. 5:21; 1 Peter 2:24).
> Jesus is not only willing to save (1 Tim. 2:4; 2 Peter 3:9),
> but He is also able to save (Heb. 7:25), and He can do it
> now (2 Cor. 6:2).
>
> Jesus encouraged the man to see the priest and to obey the
> rules for restoration given in Leviticus 14. The ceremony
> is a picture of the work of Jesus Christ in His incarnation,
> His death, and His resurrection. All of this was done over
> running water, a symbol of the Holy Spirit of God. This
> sacrifice reminds us that Jesus had to die for us in order to
> deliver us from our sins.
>
> —*Be Compassionate*, page 62

6. Why did Jesus tell the man He'd healed not to reveal who had healed
him? What did the man do instead? Why wouldn't Jesus want the publicity?
What does this little scene tell us about God's power to heal? About man's
response to God's power?

From the Commentary

Jesus returned to Capernaum, possibly to Peter's house, and the crowd gathered to see Him heal and to hear Him teach. But a new element was added: Some of the official religious leaders from Jerusalem were present to investigate what He was doing. They had every right to do this since it was the responsibility of the elders to prevent false prophets from leading the people astray (Deut. 13; 18:15–22). They had interrogated John the Baptist (John 1:19–34), and now they would examine Jesus of Nazareth.

Since this is the first time the scribes and Pharisees are mentioned in Luke's gospel, it would be good for us to get acquainted with them. The word *Pharisee* comes from a Hebrew word that means "to divide, to separate." The scribes and Pharisees probably developed out of the ministry of Ezra, the priest, who taught the Jewish people to obey the law of Moses and be separate from the heathen nations around them (Ezra 9—10; Neh. 8—9). The great desire of the scribes and Pharisees was to understand and magnify God's law and apply it in their daily lives.

However, the movement soon became quite legalistic, and its leaders laid so many burdens on the people that it was impossible to "serve the Lord with gladness" (Ps. 100:2). Furthermore, many of the Pharisees were hypocrites and did not practice what they preached (see Matt. 15:1–20; 23:1–36). In the Sermon on the Mount (Matt. 5—7), Jesus exposed the shallowness of pharisaical religion. He

explained that true righteousness is a matter of the heart
and not external religious practices alone.

—*Be Compassionate*, pages 62–63

7. Review Luke 5:17–26. How was the appearance of the Pharisees and
scribes notable at this time in Jesus' ministry? What did they get to observe
in this event? What shocking thing did Jesus do for the man with palsy?
How might the religious leaders have responded to such an act? How did
this set in motion the events that led to Jesus' arrest?

From the Commentary

The paralytic was unable to come to Jesus himself, but he
was fortunate enough to have four friends who were able
to get him to Jesus. These four men are examples of how
friends ought to minister to one another and help needy
sinners come to the Savior.

To begin with, they had faith that Jesus would heal him
(Luke 5:20), and it is faith that God honors. Their love
for the man united them in their efforts so that nothing
discouraged them, not even the crowd at the door. (How

tragic it is when spectators stand in the way of people who want to meet Jesus. Zaccheus would have this problem. See Luke 19:3.) When they could not get in at the door, they went on the roof, removed the tiling, and lowered the man on his mat right in front of the Lord!

Jesus could have simply healed the man and sent him home, but instead, He used the opportunity to teach a lesson about sin and forgiveness. Certainly it was easier to say to the man, "Your sins be forgiven!" than it was to say, "Rise up and walk!" Why? *Because nobody could prove whether or not his sins really were forgiven!* Jesus took the harder approach and healed the man's body, something everybody in the house could witness.

Was the man's affliction the result of his sin? We do not know, but it is probable (see John 5:1–14).

—Be Compassionate, pages 63–64

8. How was Jesus' healing of the man's body outward evidence of the spiritual healing within? Why are both important in this event? How was Jesus' claim to be able to forgive sin different from His claims of authority to teach and to cast out demons (Luke 4:32, 36)? How was it similar?

*More to Consider: In Luke 5:24, we have the first recorded use of
the title Son of Man in Luke's gospel, where it is found twenty-three
times. The same title was used of the prophet Ezekiel over eighty times.
The title is found at least eighty-two times in the gospel record. Why
would Jesus use this particular title for Himself? How does it differ
from "Son of God" (Matt. 27:43; Luke 22:70; John 5:25; 10:36;
11:4)? How was Jesus like Ezekiel, the Old Testament "son of man"?
(See Ezek. 3:16.)*

From the Commentary

When Jesus called Levi, He accomplished three things:
He saved a lost soul; He added a new disciple to His band;
and He created an opportunity to explain His ministry to
Levi's friends and to the scribes and Pharisees. This event
probably took place shortly after Jesus healed the palsied
man, for the "official committee" was still there (Luke
5:17). And it is likely that Jesus at this time gave Levi his
new name—"Matthew, the gift of God" (Luke 6:15; see
also Matt. 9:9).

Matthew sat at the toll booth and levied duty on the mer-
chandise that was brought through. Since the tax rates
were not always clear, it was easy for an unscrupulous
man to make extra money for himself. But even if a tax
collector served honestly, the Jews still despised him for
defiling himself by working for the Gentiles. John the
Baptist had made it clear that there was nothing innately
sinful in collecting taxes (Luke 3:12–13), and we have no

evidence that Matthew was a thief. But to the Jews, Levi was a sinner, and Jesus was suspect for having anything to do with him and his sinner friends.

—*Be Compassionate*, page 65

9. Review Luke 5:27–39. Why is it so notable that Jesus called a tax collector to be among His disciples? Who are today's "tax collectors," in terms of how society views them? What message was Jesus giving the culture by choosing an obvious "sinner" to join His small tribe of followers? What message was Jesus giving us today through this small act?

From the Commentary

The scribes and Pharisees saw Matthew and his friends as condemned sinners, but Jesus saw them as spiritually sick "patients" who needed the help of a physician. In fact, He had illustrated this when He cleansed the leper and healed the paralytic. Sin is like a disease: It starts in a small and hidden way; it grows secretly; it saps our strength; and if it is not cured, it kills. It is tragic when sickness kills the body, but it is even more tragic when sin condemns the soul to hell.

—*Be Compassionate*, page 66

10. Why were scribes and Pharisees always quick to diagnose the needs of others? In what ways were they blind to their own needs? Name some sins that morally upright people can be blind to. (For example, holding grudges.) What can a person do about his or her blind spots?

Looking Inward

Take a moment to reflect on all that you've explored thus far in this study of Luke 5. Review your notes and answers and think about how each of these things matters in your life today.

Tips for Small Groups: To get the most out of this section, form pairs or trios and have group members take turns answering these questions. Be honest and as open as you can in this discussion, but most of all, be encouraging and supportive of others. Be sensitive to those who are going through particularly difficult times and don't press for people to speak if they're uncomfortable doing so.

11. Have you ever treated someone as the Jews treated the lepers in Jesus' day? Explain. What made you so uncomfortable around this person? How might Jesus have interacted with this person?

12. Do you believe God performs healing miracles today? Why or why not? Have you ever been on the receiving end of a healing miracle? Or have you ever witnessed one? Describe the circumstance. How did you know this was a God-thing and not just coincidence or a medical anomaly?

13. Are you like the scribes and Pharisees in any way? What are some of the ways you try to look good on the outside, regardless of the condition of your heart? Why do you try to look good to others? What drives that desire? What are the challenges of dealing with the truth of your heart?

Going Forward

14. Think of one or two things that you have learned that you'd like to work on in the coming week. Remember that this is all about quality, not quantity. It's better to work on one specific area of life and do it well than to work on many and do poorly (or to be so overwhelmed that you simply don't try).

Do you want to deal with the truth of your heart? Be specific. Go back through Luke 5 and put a star next to the phrase or verse that is most encouraging to you. Consider memorizing this verse.

Real-Life Application Ideas: This week, be intentional in reaching out to the people in your life who are suffering from illness—whether physical, emotional, psychological, or even spiritual. Visit the sick and pray for them. Offer to listen to those who suffer from a broken heart or broken spirit. And all along the way, ask God to use you to help in the healing process, however He wills.

Seeking Help

15. Write a prayer below (or simply pray one in silence), inviting God to work on your mind and heart in those areas you've noted in the Going Forward section. Be honest about your desires and fears.

Notes for Small Groups:
- *Look for ways to put into practice the things you wrote in the Going Forward section above. Talk with other group members about your ideas and commit to being accountable to one another.*
- *During the coming week, ask the Holy Spirit to continue to reveal truth to you from what you've read and studied.*
- *Before you start the next lesson, read Luke 6—7. For more in-depth lesson preparation, read chapters 5, "So What's New? Everything!," and 6, "Compassion in Action," in* Be Compassionate.

 All Things New
LUKE 6—7

Before you begin ...
- *Pray for the Holy Spirit to reveal truth and wisdom as you go through this lesson.*
- *Read Luke 6—7. This lesson references chapters 5 and 6 in* Be Compassionate. *It will be helpful for you to have your Bible and a copy of the commentary available as you work through this lesson.*

Getting Started

From the Commentary

The sanctity of the seventh day was a distinctive part of the Jewish faith. God gave Israel the Sabbath law at Sinai (Neh. 9:13–14) and made it a sign between Him and the nation (Ex. 20:8–11; 31:12–17). The word *Sabbath* means "rest" and is linked with God's cessation of work after the six days of creation (Gen. 2:2–3). Some of the rabbis taught that Messiah could not come until Israel had

perfectly kept the Sabbath, so obeying this law was very
important both personally and nationally.

—*Be Compassionate*, page 73

1. Review Luke 6:1–11. What reasons for the Sabbath did God give in
Exodus 20:8–11? What would periodically resting from work have
communicated to the people? How is this distinct from the day of the
week we call Sunday or the Lord's Day (see Matt. 28:1–7; Acts 20:7; Rev.
1:10)? What does the Lord's Day commemorate? Does it matter which day
of the week we commemorate? Why or why not?

*More to Consider: The early church met on the first day of the week
(Acts 20:7; 1 Cor. 16:1–2). However, some Jewish believers kept the
Sabbath, and this sometimes led to division. Read Romans 14:1—
15:13. How did Paul address this problem? How did Paul define the
relationship (or lack thereof) between the Sabbath and salvation? (See
Gal. 4:1–11; Col. 2:8–17.)*

2. Choose one verse or phrase from Luke 6—7 that stands out to you.
This could be something you're intrigued by, something that makes you

uncomfortable, something that puzzles you, something that resonates with you, or just something you want to examine further. Write that here.

Going Deeper

From the Commentary

> The Pharisees knew that it was our Lord's practice to be in the synagogue on the Sabbath, so they were there to watch Him and to gather more evidence against Him. Did they know that the handicapped man would also be there? Did they "plant" him there? We do not know, and Jesus probably did not care. His compassionate heart responded to the man's need, and He healed him. Jesus could have waited a few hours until the Sabbath was over, or He could have healed the man in private, but He did it openly and immediately. It was a deliberate violation of the Sabbath traditions.
>
> Our Lord's defense in the field was based on the Old Testament Scriptures, but His defense in the synagogue was based on *the nature of God's Sabbath law.* God gave that law to help people, not to hurt them. "The sabbath was made for man, and not man for the sabbath"

(Mark 2:27). Every man in the synagogue would rescue a sheep on the Sabbath, so why not rescue a man made in the image of God (Matt. 12:11–12)? The scribes and Pharisees had turned God's gift into a heavy yoke that nobody could bear (Acts 15:10; Gal. 5:1).

This miracle illustrates the power of faith in God's Word.

—*Be Compassionate*, pages 75–76

3. Review Luke 6:6–11. How does this miracle illustrate the power of faith in God's Word? Why would this be controversial to the scribes and Pharisees? How did Jesus defend His actions in the synagogue? (See Mark 2:27; Matt. 12:11–12.) In what ways had the scribes and Pharisees turned God's gift of the Sabbath into a burden?

From the Commentary

Jesus spent the whole night in prayer, for He was about to call His twelve apostles from among the many disciples who were following Him. A *disciple* is a learner, an apprentice; while an *apostle* is a chosen messenger sent with a special commission. Jesus had many disciples (see Luke 10:1) but only twelve handpicked apostles.

—Be Compassionate, pages 76–77

4. Why did Jesus pray all night? What does this say about the task He was facing? About His knowledge of the growing opposition against Him? How did the fact that Jesus was fully human impact these sorts of emotional moments? (See Luke 22:41–44; Heb. 5:7–8.)

From the Commentary

The sermon in 6:20–49 is probably a shorter version of what we call "The Sermon on the Mount" (Matt. 5—7), though some fine evangelical scholars believe these were two different events. If they are the same event, the fact that Matthew locates it on a mountain (Matt. 5:1), while Luke puts it "in the plain" (Luke 6:17), creates no problem. Dr. D. A. Carson points out that the Greek word translated "plain" can mean "a plateau in a mountainous region" (*Exegetical Fallacies,* Baker, 43).

Jesus went "into the hill country" with His disciples. After a night of prayer, He came down to a level place, ordained the Twelve, ministered to the sick, and then preached this sermon. It was His description of what it means to have a life of "blessing."

To most Jewish people, the word *blessing* evoked images of a long life; wealth; a large, healthy family; a full barn; and defeated enemies. God's covenant with Israel did include such material and physical blessings (Deut. 28; Job 1:1–12; Prov. 3:1–10), for this was how God taught and disciplined them. After all, they were "little children" . in the faith, and we teach children by means of rewards and punishments. With the coming of Jesus, Israel's childhood period ended, and the people had to mature in their understanding of God's ways (Gal. 4:1–6).

—*Be Compassionate*, pages 78–79

5. Review Luke 6:20–49. In what ways were Jesus' messages as much for His disciples as for the multitudes? What might the disciples have had to unlearn as they followed Jesus? What are some aspects of this teaching that go against the common beliefs and practices of our culture?

From the Commentary

> Jesus assumed that anybody who lived for eternal values would get into trouble with the world's crowd. Christians are the "salt of the earth" and "the light of the world" (Matt. 5:13–16), and sometimes the salt stings and the light exposes sin. Sinners show their hatred by avoiding us or rejecting us (Luke 6:22), insulting us (Luke 6:28), physically abusing us (Luke 6:29), and suing us (Luke 6:30). This is something we must expect (Phil. 1:29; 2 Tim. 3:12).
>
> —*Be Compassionate*, pages 81–82

6. Why was Jesus' message about how we're to treat our enemies revolutionary? How do Jesus' admonitions speak to what goes on inside us, not just to rules for outward behavior? What role does the Holy Spirit ultimately play in our ability to treat our enemies with love? (See Rom. 5:5; Gal. 5:22–23.) What role does discernment play in how we're to love others? (See Phil. 1:9–11.)

From the Commentary

In the Gospels and the book of Acts, Roman centurions are presented as quality men of character, and Luke 7:1–10 reveals a sterling example of this. The Jewish elders had little love for the Romans in general and Roman soldiers in particular, and yet the elders commended this officer to Jesus. He loved the Jewish people in Capernaum and even built them a synagogue. He loved his servant and did not want him to die. This centurion was not a Stoic who insulated himself from the pain of others. He had a heart of concern, even for his lowly servant boy who was dying from a paralyzing disease (Matt. 8:6).

Matthew's condensed report (Matt. 8:5–13) does not contradict Luke's fuller account. The centurion's friends represented him to Jesus and then represented Jesus to him. When a newscaster reports that the president or the prime minister said something to Congress or Parliament, this does not necessarily mean that the message was delivered by them in person. It was probably delivered by one of their official representatives, but the message would be received as from the president or prime minister personally.

We are impressed not only with this man's great love, but also his great humility. Imagine a Roman officer telling a poor Jewish rabbi that he was unworthy to have Him enter his house! The Romans were not known for displaying humility, especially before their Jewish subjects.

—Be Compassionate, pages 89–90

7. What most impressed Jesus about the Roman officer? What does it mean that Jesus was "amazed"? (See also Mark 6:6.) Jesus also commended a Gentile woman whose daughter He delivered from a demon (Matt. 15:28). Is it significant that in both of these instances, Jesus healed at a distance? (See Ps. 107:20; Eph. 2:11–13.) What does this say to us today about Jesus? About God's ability to heal? About faith?

From the Commentary

Nain was about twenty-five miles from Capernaum, a good day's journey away, yet Jesus went there even though He was not requested to come. Since the Jews buried their dead the same day (Deut. 21:23; Acts 5:5–10), it is likely that Jesus and His disciples arrived at the city gate late in the afternoon of the day the boy died. Four special meetings took place at the city gate that day.

(1) Two crowds met. We can only marvel at the providence of God when we see Jesus meet that funeral procession just as it was heading for the burial ground. He lived on a divine timetable as He obeyed the will of His Father (John 11:9; 13:1). The sympathetic Savior always gives help when we need it most (Heb. 4:16).

(2) Two only sons met. One was alive but destined to die, the other dead but destined to live. The term *only begotten* as applied to Jesus means "unique," "the only one of its kind." Jesus is not a "son" in the same sense that I am, having been brought into existence by conception and birth. Since Jesus is eternal God, He has always existed. The title *Son of God* declares Christ's divine nature and His relationship to the Father, to whom the Son has willingly subjected Himself from all eternity. All the Persons of the Godhead are equal, but in the "economy" of the Trinity, each has a specific place to fill and task to fulfill.

(3) Two sufferers met. Jesus, "the man of sorrows," could easily identify with the widow's heartache. Not only was she in sorrow, but she was now left alone in a society that did not have resources to care for widows. What would happen to her? Jesus felt the pain that sin and death have brought into this world, and He did something about it.

(4) Two enemies met. Jesus faced death, "the last enemy" (1 Cor. 15:26). When you consider the pain and grief that it causes in this world, death is indeed an enemy, and only Jesus Christ can give us victory (see 1 Cor. 15:51–58; Heb. 2:14–15). Jesus had only to speak the word, and the boy was raised to life and health.

—*Be Compassionate*, pages 91–92

8. Review Luke 7:11–17. How would you compare this miracle to Jesus' earlier ones? What does it reveal about Him? What was the people's response to this miracle? (See Deut. 18:15; John 1:21; Acts 3:22–23.) How

accurate was their understanding of Jesus? What was the result of this miracle (Luke 8:4, 19, 42)?

From the Commentary

> John had been in prison some months (Luke 3:19–20), but he knew what Jesus was doing because his own disciples kept him informed. It must have been difficult for this man, accustomed to a wilderness life, to be confined in a prison. The physical and emotional strain were no doubt great, and the long days of waiting did not make it easier. The Jewish leaders did nothing to intercede for John, and it seemed that even Jesus was doing nothing for him. If He came to set the prisoners free (Luke 4:18), then John the Baptist was a candidate!
>
> —*Be Compassionate*, page 93

9. What is the difference between doubt and unbelief? What are other examples of doubt in Scripture? (See Num. 11:10–15; 1 Kings 19; Jer. 20:7–9, 14–18; and 2 Cor. 1:8–9.) How are those situations similar to or

different from John's? In what ways is unbelief a matter of the will? Why does the distinction between doubt and unbelief matter?

More to Consider: The Greek word translated "offended" gives us our English word scandalize, *and it referred originally to the "bait stick" in a trap. How was John in danger of being trapped because of his concern about what Jesus was not doing? How did Jesus respond to this concern? How does He respond to the same concerns we have today when we think God isn't acting quickly enough or decisively enough in our own stories?*

From the Commentary

Jesus not only accepted hospitality from the publicans and sinners but also from the Pharisees. They needed the Word of God too, whether they realized it or not. We trust that Simon's invitation was a sincere one and that he did not have some ulterior motive for having Jesus in his home. If he did, his plan backfired, because he ended up learning more about himself than he cared to know!

The repentant woman (vv. 36–38). It was customary in that day for outsiders to hover around during banquets so they could watch the "important people" and hear the conversation. Since everything was open, they could even enter the banquet hall and speak to a guest. This explains how this woman had access to Jesus. He was not behind locked doors. In that day women were not invited to banquets.

Jewish rabbis did not speak to women in public, nor did they eat with them in public. A woman of this type would not be welcomed in the house of Simon the Pharisee. Her sins are not named, but we get the impression she was a woman of the streets with a bad reputation.

The critical host (vv. 39–43). Simon was embarrassed, both for himself and for his guests. People had been saying that Jesus was a great prophet (Luke 7:16), but He certainly was not exhibiting much prophetic discernment if He allowed a sinful woman to anoint His feet! He must be a fraud.

The forgiving Savior (vv. 44–50). The woman was guilty of sins of commission, but Simon was guilty of sins of omission. He had not been a gracious host to the Lord Jesus.

—*Be Compassionate*, pages 96–97

10. What was Simon's real problem? How did Jesus prove He was a prophet in His response to Simon? What is the difference between sins of commission and sins of omission? What are the similarities?

Looking Inward

Take a moment to reflect on all that you've explored thus far in this study of Luke 6—7. Review your notes and answers and think about how each of these things matters in your life today.

> *Tips for Small Groups: To get the most out of this section, form pairs or trios and have group members take turns answering these questions. Be honest and as open as you can in this discussion, but most of all, be encouraging and supportive of others. Be sensitive to those who are going through particularly difficult times and don't press for people to speak if they're uncomfortable doing so.*

11. Jesus prayed all night when He was facing a challenging day. What do you do when you know you're facing a difficult event in life? How does prayer fit into your preparation for challenges? How can it help you face those challenges?

12. Describe a time when you experienced doubt in God. How was that like and unlike any seasons of unbelief you've known? Does doubting cause you distress or concern? Explain. How can God use your doubt to bring you closer to Him?

13. What are some ways you've committed sins of omission? Are those harder or easier to acknowledge than sins of commission? Why? How do sins of omission affect your relationship with others? With Jesus?

Going Forward

14. Think of one or two things that you have learned that you'd like to work on in the coming week. Remember that this is all about quality, not quantity. It's better to work on one specific area of life and do it well than to work on many and do poorly (or to be so overwhelmed that you simply don't try).

Do you want to better understand and deal with your seasons of doubt? Be specific. Go back through Luke 6—7 and put a star next to the phrase or verse that is most encouraging to you. Consider memorizing this verse.

Real-Life Application Ideas: Much of Jesus' earthly ministry involved showing compassion toward those whom the culture might otherwise ignore or even disparage. This week, make a plan to perform specific acts of compassion toward others. This could be helping a coworker with a difficult project, cleaning a neighbor's yard, preparing a meal for a friend, or simply taking time out of your day to listen to a lonely stranger.

Seeking Help

15. Write a prayer below (or simply pray one in silence), inviting God to work on your mind and heart in those areas you've noted in the Going Forward section. Be honest about your desires and fears.

Notes for Small Groups:

- *Look for ways to put into practice the things you wrote in the Going Forward section. Talk with other group members about your ideas and commit to being accountable to one another.*

- *During the coming week, ask the Holy Spirit to continue to reveal truth to you from what you've read and studied.*

- *Before you start the next lesson, read Luke 8. For more in-depth lesson preparation, read chapter 7, "Lessons about Faith," in* Be Compassionate.

Faith Lessons
LUKE 8

Before you begin ...
- *Pray for the Holy Spirit to reveal truth and wisdom as you go through this lesson.*
- *Read Luke 8. This lesson references chapter 7 in* Be Compassionate. *It will be helpful for you to have your Bible and a copy of the commentary available as you work through this lesson.*

Getting Started

From the Commentary

One of the major themes in Luke 8 is how to get faith and use it in the everyday experiences of life. In the first section, Jesus laid the foundation by teaching His disciples that faith comes through receiving the Word of God into an understanding heart. In the second part, He put them through a series of "examinations" to see how much they had really learned. Most of us enjoy Bible study, but we wish we could avoid the examinations that often follow the lessons! However, it is in the tests of life that faith really grows and we get closer to Christ.

The cynical American editor H. L. Mencken defined faith as "an illogical belief in the occurrence of the impossible," and Mark Twain said (through one of his characters) that faith is "believin' what you know ain't so." Of course, these men are describing superstition, not faith, for the faith of a Christian rests on solid foundations.

—*Be Compassionate*, page 103

1. In what ways does everyone live by faith in someone or something? What's the difference between those who live by faith in Christ and those who live by faith in something else? Why is the "object" of our faith important to how we live?

2. Choose one verse or phrase from Luke 8 that stands out to you. This could be something you're intrigued by, something that makes you uncomfortable, something that puzzles you, something that resonates with you, or just something you want to examine further. Write that here.

Going Deeper

From the Commentary

> The Lord continued His itinerant ministry in Galilee, assisted by His disciples and partially supported by some godly women. It was not unusual for Jewish rabbis to receive gifts from grateful people, and these women had certainly benefited from Jesus' ministry. The New Testament church leaders were supported by gifts from friends (2 Tim. 1:16–18) and from churches (Phil. 4:15–17), and Paul supported himself by his own labor (2 Thess. 3:6–10).
>
> —*Be Compassionate*, page 104

3. Underline all the uses of the word *hear* in Luke 8:1–21. What does hearing mean in a spiritual context? How do we "hear" today? What obstacles are there to hearing? How can we overcome those obstacles?

More to Consider: Respond to the following statement by A. W. Tozer: "Faith comes first to the hearing ear, not to the cogitating mind." What role does hearing play in our faith? (See James 1:22–25.) What role does the mind play? The heart?

From the Commentary

In the parable in 8:4–15, the sower is initially Jesus Christ, but the sower also represents any of God's people who share the Word of God (John 4:35–38). The seed is the Word of God, for, like seed, the Word has life and power (Heb. 4:12) and can produce spiritual fruit (Gal. 5:22–23). But the seed can do nothing until it is planted (John 12:24). When a person hears and understands the Word, then the seed is planted in the heart. What happens after that depends on the nature of the soil.

Jesus called this parable "the parable of the sower" (Matt. 13:18), but it could also be called "the parable of the soils." The seed without the soil is fruitless, and the soil without the seed is almost useless. The human heart is like soil: If it is prepared properly, it can receive the seed of the Word of God and produce a fruitful harvest.

Jesus described four different kinds of hearts, three of which did not produce any fruit. The proof of salvation is *fruit* and not merely hearing the Word or making a profession of faith in Christ. Jesus had already made that clear in His "Sermon on the Mount" (Luke 6:43–49; also note Matt. 7:20).

—*Be Compassionate*, page 104

4. What do the different kinds of soil represent in this parable? What does this parable tell us about Jesus' feelings about the big crowd that followed Him? What message was He giving to His disciples about their own ministry to come?

From Today's World

Jesus often spoke in parables when He was talking to His disciples, but also when He was talking to the multitudes. Through the use of culturally relevant stories, He revealed spiritually relevant truths. While we rarely hear parables in modern culture, the role that stories play is at least as significant to our culture, if not more so. Consider the influence of movies, books, television shows, and even music. While much of what our culture ingests through these mediums is entertainment, just as in parables there is often a message (with greater or lesser degrees of truth) to be discovered in the fiction.

5. Jesus knew the power of a story. How do stories today continue to influence our beliefs and understanding of the world? What does this tell us about being wise about what to watch or listen to? How can we use stories to share God's truth today? What are some ways artists, actors, writers, and musicians are doing that very thing?

From the Commentary

The disciples were perplexed because Jesus taught in parables, so they asked Him for an explanation (Luke 8:9–10; also see Matt. 13:10–17). His reply seems to suggest that He used parables in order to *hide* the truth from the crowds, but just the opposite is true, and Luke 8:16–18 makes that clear. His teaching is a light that must be allowed to shine so that sinners may be saved.

The word *parable* means "to cast alongside." A parable is a story that teaches something new by putting the truth alongside something familiar. The people knew about seeds and soil, so the parable of the sower interested them. Those who were indifferent or proud would shrug it off. Our Lord's parables aroused the interest of the concerned.

A parable starts off as a *picture* that is familiar to the listeners. But as you carefully consider the picture, it becomes a *mirror* in which you see yourself, and many people do not like to see themselves. This explains why some of our Lord's listeners became angry when they heard His parables, and even tried to kill Him. But if we see ourselves as needy sinners and ask for help, then the mirror becomes a *window* through which we see God and His grace. To understand a parable and benefit from it demands honesty and humility on our part, and many of our Lord's hearers lacked both.

—*Be Compassionate*, pages 106–7

6. Why is hearing the Word of God a serious thing? Why would Jesus expect and desire listeners to think about what's being said rather than simply know it well enough to recycle the words? In what ways do hearers become sowers? What does this say about the importance of understanding God's Word? What happens if we don't "get it" and yet try to share it?

From the Commentary

By the time the Lord had finished giving "the parables of the kingdom" (Matt. 13:1–52), the disciples must have felt like postgraduate students in the School of Faith! They now understood mysteries that were hidden from the scribes and rabbis and even from the Old Testament prophets. What they did not realize (and we are so like them!) is *that faith must be tested before it can be trusted.* It is one thing to learn a new spiritual truth, but quite something else to practice that truth in the everyday experiences of life.

Truth that is only in the head is purely academic and never will get into the heart until it is practiced by the will.

—*Be Compassionate*, page 108

7. Review Luke 8:22–56. Respond to this statement: Satan does not care how much Bible truth we learn so long as we do not live it. What does God want from His children when it comes to matters of knowledge and information (Eph. 1:17–19; 6:6; James 1:22)? How do we put our knowledge into action?

From the Commentary

Jesus was weary from a long day of teaching and went to sleep as the ship left Capernaum for the opposite shore. But before He did, He gave them a word of command that was also a word of promise: They were going to the opposite shore. This word should have encouraged and strengthened the disciples during the storm, but their faith was still small (Matt. 8:26).

While our tour group was sailing from Tiberias to Capernaum, I asked our guide if he had ever been in a storm on the Sea of Galilee. His eyes opened wide and he said, "Yes, and I hope it never happens to me again!" The situation is such that sudden squalls occur as winds from the mountains funnel to the lake located six hundred feet below sea level. When the cold air and warm air meet in this natural basin, a storm is sure to develop.

The disciples were afraid, *but Jesus was not!* He kept on sleeping, confident that His Father was completely in control (Ps. 89:8–9). The disciples became so frightened that they awakened Him and begged Him to rescue them. The title *Master* is the same one Peter used in Luke 5:5. Of course, their problem was not the storm around them but the unbelief within them.

—*Be Compassionate*, pages 108–9

8. Read Luke 4:35, 41; 9:42. How do these uses of "rebuke" compare to what Jesus said to the storm? In what ways was the disciples' unbelief more dangerous than the storm? In what ways does this event reveal truth about God's active role in the world? About the manner in which He chooses to control events for His purposes?

More to Consider: Did Jesus have the right to permit the legion of demons to destroy a herd of two thousand swine and perhaps put the owners out of business? Explain. (See Ps. 50:10–11; Matt. 12:12.) Why did the community beg Jesus to leave instead of thank Him? How is this like the way we react to God when His actions seem to contradict our wishes?

From the Commentary

When Jesus returned to Capernaum, the people welcomed Him, particularly a man and a woman who each had heavy burdens to share with Jesus. The contrast here is interesting, for it shows the variety of people who came to Jesus for help. The man's name is given (Jairus), but the woman is anonymous. Jairus was a wealthy leading citizen, but the woman was a lowly person who had spent all her money trying to get well. Here was a man interceding for his child and a woman hoping to get help for herself, and both came to the feet of Jesus. Jairus had been blessed with twelve years of joy with his daughter, and now might lose her, while the woman had experienced twelve years of misery because of her affliction, and now she was hoping to get well.

This woman had a hidden need, a burden she had lived with for twelve long years. It affected her physically and made life difficult. But it also affected her spiritually, because the hemorrhage made her ceremonially defiled and unable to participate in the religious life of the nation (Lev. 15:19–22). She was defiled, destitute, discouraged, and desperate, but she came to Jesus and her need was met.

—*Be Compassionate*, page 111

9. In what way was the woman's faith almost superstitious? Why did Jesus honor that faith anyway? What are some of the "hidden needs" that we bring to Jesus today?

From the Commentary

When Jairus left home, his daughter was so sick she was ready to die. By the time Jesus got away from the crowd to go with him, the girl had died. Jairus's friends thought that Jesus could help only living people, so they advised Jairus to drop the matter and come home. But Jesus encouraged the distraught father with a word of hope.

The scene at the home would have discouraged anybody! The professional mourners were already there, weeping and wailing, and a crowd of friends and neighbors had gathered. Jewish people in that day lost no time or energy in showing and sharing their grief. The body of the deceased would be buried that same day, after being washed and anointed.

Jesus took command of the situation and told the crowd to stop weeping because the girl was not dead but asleep. Of course she was dead, for her spirit had left her body (compare Luke 8:55 with James 2:26), but to Jesus, death was only sleep. This image is often used in the New Testament to describe the death of believers (John 11:11–14; Acts 7:59–60; 1 Cor. 15:51; 1 Thess. 4:13–18). Sleep is a normal experience that we do not fear, and we should not fear death. It is the body that sleeps, not the spirit, for the spirit of the believer goes to be with Christ (Phil. 1:20–24; 2 Cor. 5:6–8). At the resurrection, the body will be "awakened" and glorified, and God's people will share the image of Christ (1 John 3:1–2).

The mourners laughed at Jesus because they knew the girl was dead and that death was final. But they failed to realize that Jesus is "the resurrection and the life" (John 11:25–26). Had He not raised the widow's son from the dead? Did He not tell John the Baptist that the dead were being raised (Luke 7:22)? Apparently the mourners did not believe these reports and thought Jesus was a fool.

So He put them all out! This situation was much too tender and special for Him to allow dozens of unbelieving spectators to watch. He took the parents and three of His disciples, Peter, James, and John, and together they entered the room where the little girl lay dead.

He took her by the hand and spoke in Aramaic, "Talitha cumi! Little girl, arise!" (Peter would one day say, "Tabitha cumi!"—Acts 9:40.) This was not a magic formula but a word of command from the Lord of life and death (Rev. 1:17–18). Her spirit returned to her body, and she arose and began to walk around the room! Jesus told them to give her something to eat, for it is likely that during her illness she had eaten little or nothing. Jesus also instructed them not to spread the news, but still the word got around (Matt. 9:26).

The Gospels record three resurrections, though Jesus probably performed more. In each instance, the person raised gave evidence of life. The widow's son began to speak (Luke 7:15), Jairus's daughter walked and ate food, and Lazarus was loosed from the graveclothes (John 11:44). When a lost sinner is raised from the dead, you can tell it by his speech, his walk, his appetite, and his "change of clothes" (Col. 3:1ff.). You cannot hide life!

—*Be Compassionate*, pages 112–14

10. Why did Jesus once again instruct the people not to spread the news of His raising of Jairus' daughter? What sort of response might Jesus have gotten if the word had spread wide? In what ways is resurrection a picture of the way Jesus saves sinners? (See John 5:24; Eph. 2:1–10.)

Looking Inward

Take a moment to reflect on all that you've explored thus far in this study of Luke 8. Review your notes and answers and think about how each of these things matters in your life today.

> *Tips for Small Groups: To get the most out of this section, form pairs or trios and have group members take turns answering these questions. Be honest and as open as you can in this discussion, but most of all, be encouraging and supportive of others. Be sensitive to those who are going through particularly difficult times and don't press for people to speak if they're uncomfortable doing so.*

11. What is your greatest struggle with faith in Jesus? When do you feel most sound in your faith? When do you feel most uncertain about it? How does your faith inform your daily life?

12. How would you characterize your knowledge of the Bible and biblical truth? What are some ways you grow that knowledge? What does it look like to put that knowledge into action? Describe some ways you apply and live out the knowledge you have.

13. How are you like Jairus or the anonymous woman who approached Jesus with a secret need? Think about some of the secret needs you have right now. How can you invite Jesus' healing in those areas of your life? How might God be able to use other people in your life to help you with those secret needs?

Going Forward

14. Think of one or two things that you have learned that you'd like to work on in the coming week. Remember that this is all about quality, not quantity. It's better to work on one specific area of life and do it well than to work on many and do poorly (or to be so overwhelmed that you simply don't try).

Do you want to better understand why you struggle with faith? Be specific. Go back through Luke 8 and put a star next to the phrase or verse that is most encouraging to you. Consider memorizing this verse.

Real-Life Application Ideas: This week, live out the parable of the sower by planting seeds of God's Word at work, at home, in your community, and even among strangers. What "planting seeds" looks like for you may look different than it does for someone else. That's okay. Perhaps you're not comfortable talking openly about your faith. If so, simply invite others to spend time with you—a dinner, bowling, a movie. Begin to build relationships with people who don't yet know Christ, and let them see Christ in you as you do. Relationship building is a great way to plant seeds. Just be ready for that moment when someone asks, "What is it that's different about you?"

Seeking Help

15. Write a prayer below (or simply pray one in silence), inviting God to work on your mind and heart in those areas you've noted in the Going Forward section. Be honest about your desires and fears.

Notes for Small Groups:

- *Look for ways to put into practice the things you wrote in the Going Forward section. Talk with other group members about your ideas and commit to being accountable to one another.*

- *During the coming week, ask the Holy Spirit to continue to reveal truth to you from what you've read and studied.*

- *Before you start the next lesson, read Luke 9—10. For more in-depth lesson preparation, read chapters 8, "A Many-Sided Ministry," and 9, "What in the World Does a Christian Do?," in* Be Compassionate.

Ministry with Purpose

LUKE 9—10

Before you begin …
- *Pray for the Holy Spirit to reveal truth and wisdom as you go through this lesson.*
- *Read Luke 9—10. This lesson references chapters 8 and 9 in* Be Compassionate. *It will be helpful for you to have your Bible and a copy of the commentary available as you work through this lesson.*

Getting Started

From the Commentary

The Twelve had been ordained some months before (Luke 6:13–16) and had been traveling with Jesus as His helpers. Now He was going to send them out in pairs (Mark 6:7) to have their own ministry and to put into practice what they had learned. This was their "solo flight."

But before He sent them out, He gave them the equipment needed to get the job done, as well as the instructions to follow. The parallel passage in Matthew 10 reveals that the Twelve were sent only to the people of Israel (Matt. 10:5–6). Luke does not mention this since he wrote primarily for the Gentiles and emphasized the worldwide outreach of the gospel.

—*Be Compassionate*, pages 117–18

1. Review Luke 9:1–6. What "tools" did Jesus give the disciples when He sent them out? What instructions did He give? What does it mean to preach the gospel? (See v. 6.)

More to Consider: Why did God give the disciples the ability to do healing miracles? (See Rom. 15:18–19; 2 Cor. 12:12; Heb. 2:1–4; Mark 16:20.) How do we test a person's ministry today? (See 1 John 2:18–29; 4:1–6.) Why are miracles not enough to prove that someone is sent by God? (See Matt. 24:24; 2 Cor. 11:13–15; 2 Thess. 2:9–10.)

2. Choose one verse or phrase from Luke 9—10 that stands out to you. This could be something you're intrigued by, something that makes you

uncomfortable, something that puzzles you, something that resonates with you, or just something you want to examine further. Write that here.

Going Deeper

From the Commentary

> Our Lord was not the kind of person who could teach the Word and then say to hungry people, "Depart in peace, be ye warmed and filled" (James 2:16). The disciples were only too eager to see the crowd leave (Luke 18:15; see Matt. 15:23). They had not yet caught the compassion of Christ and the burden He had for the multitudes, but one day they would.
>
> When you combine all four accounts of this miracle, you find that Jesus first asked Philip where they could buy enough bread to feed such a great crowd. (There could well have been ten thousand people there.) He was only testing Philip, "for He Himself knew what He was intending to do" (John 6:6 NASB). In the crisis hours of life, when your resources are low and your responsibilities are great, it is good to remember that God already has the problem solved. Jesus started with what they had, a few

loaves and fishes that were generously donated by a lad found by Andrew (John 6:8–9). Did Andrew know the boy? Or did the boy offer his little lunch without being asked? Before we ask God to do the impossible, let's start with the possible and give Him what we have. And while we are at it, let's give thanks for mothers who give their sons something to give to Jesus.

—*Be Compassionate*, page 120

3. Why did Jesus look up to heaven to give thanks for the food before performing this miracle? (See Matt. 6:11.) What did this teach His followers about provision? What does the fact that there were so many leftovers tell us about Jesus? What should we do today if we feel that God isn't multiplying the loaves for us?

From the Commentary

In Luke's gospel, the feeding of the five thousand marks the end of what is called the "Great Galilean Ministry" (Luke 4:14—9:17). Jesus now begins His journey to Jerusalem (see Luke 9:51; 13:22; 17:11; 18:31; 19:11, 28).

This would be a time of relative retirement with His disciples as He prepared them for what lay ahead. There is a parallel between this account and the account in Acts of Paul's last journey to Jerusalem. In both books we have "a tale of two cities": in Luke, from Nazareth to Jerusalem; and in Acts, from Jerusalem to Rome.

If any of us asked our friends what people were saying about us, it would be an evidence of pride, but not so with Jesus Christ. People had better know who He is, because what we think about Jesus determines our eternal destiny (John 8:24; 1 John 4:1–3). It is impossible to be wrong about Jesus and right with God.

Jesus had prayed all night before choosing His disciples (Luke 6:12–13), and now He prayed before asking for their personal confession of faith. The crowd would have its opinions (see Luke 9:7–8), but His disciples must have convictions. Peter was the spokesman for the group and gave a clear witness to the deity of Jesus Christ. This was the second time that he confessed Christ publicly (John 6:68–69). Except for Judas (John 6:70–71), all of the Twelve had faith in Jesus Christ.

—Be Compassionate, pages 121–22

4. Review Luke 9:18–21. Jesus commanded His disciples not to spread the truth. Why? What did He expect of His disciples? Why didn't He ask them for their confession of faith sooner?

From the Commentary

> Jesus had already given a number of "hints" about His sacrificial death, but now He began to teach this truth clearly to His disciples. John the Baptist had presented Him as the "Lamb of God" (John 1:29), and Jesus had predicted the "destruction" of the temple of His body (John 2:19). When He compared Himself to the serpent in the wilderness (John 3:14) and to Jonah (Matt. 12:38–40), Jesus was making statements about His suffering and death.
>
> This is the first of three statements in Luke about His coming passion in Jerusalem (Luke 9:43–45; 18:31–34). It is clear that the Twelve did not understand, partly because of their unbelief and immaturity, and partly because it was "hidden" from them by God. Jesus taught them as they were able to receive the truth (John 16:12). It must have shocked the men to hear that their own religious leaders would kill their Master.
>
> But Jesus did not stop with a private announcement of His own death. He also made a public declaration about a cross for *every* disciple.
>
> —*Be Compassionate*, page 122

5. Read 9:22–26. This is the first of three statements in Luke about Jesus' coming passion in Jerusalem (see also 9:43–45; 18:31–34). What was the response of the disciples to this statement? Why didn't they

understand? Why did Jesus also make a public declaration about a cross for every disciple? What did He mean? Why did the disciples want to disbelieve this news?

From the Commentary

As far as the gospel record is concerned, the transfiguration was the only occasion during Christ's earthly ministry when He revealed the glory of His person. Luke did not use the word *transfigure*, but he described the same scene (Matt. 17:2; Mark 9:2). The word means "a change in appearance that comes from within," and it gives us the English word *metamorphosis*.

What were the reasons behind this event? For one thing, it was God's seal of approval to Peter's confession of faith that Jesus is the Son of God (John 1:14). It was also the Father's way of encouraging the Son as He began to make His way to Jerusalem. The Father had spoken at the baptism (Luke 3:22) and would speak again during that final week of the Son's earthly ministry (John 12:23–28). Beyond the suffering of the cross would be the glory of the throne, a lesson that Peter emphasized in his first epistle (1 Peter 4:12—5:4).

Our Lord's own words in Luke 9:27 indicate that the event was a demonstration (or illustration) of the promised kingdom of God. This seems logical, for the disciples were confused about the kingdom because of Jesus' words about the cross. (We must not be too hard on them, because the prophets were also confused—1 Peter 1:10–12.)

—*Be Compassionate*, page 124

6. What was the purpose of the transfiguration event? How did the transfiguration reveal Jesus' glory? What are some ways we can have a spiritual transfiguration experience each day as we walk with the Lord?

From the Commentary

"How long shall I stay with you and put up with you?" (Luke 9:41 NIV) You might expect that lament to come from an overworked kindergarten teacher or an impatient army drill instructor, but it was made by the sinless Son of

God! We are prone to forget how long-suffering our Lord had to be while He was ministering on earth, especially with His own disciples.

—*Be Compassionate*, page 126

7. Review Luke 9:41. What prompted Jesus to speak these words to His disciples? What event in this section gave Jesus a reason to be disappointed in them? What are other reasons Jesus was grieved by His followers?

From the Commentary

The event in 10:1–24 should not be confused with the sending out of the Twelve (Matt. 10; Luke 9:1–11). There are similarities in the charges given, but this is to be expected since both groups were sent by the same Master to do the same basic job. The twelve apostles ministered throughout Galilee, but these men were sent into Judea, and the men in this chapter are not called apostles. They were anonymous disciples.

—*Be Compassionate*, pages 131

8. What details in Luke 10:1–16 give it a sense of urgency? Why was the matter so urgent? Is it still urgent? Why or why not? What are the implications for us?

More to Consider: It is important to note that the special power that Jesus gave to His apostles (Luke 9:1) and to the seventy is not ours to claim today. These two preaching missions were very special ministries, and God did not promise to duplicate them in our age. Our Lord's commission to us emphasizes the proclamation of the message, not the performing of miracles (Matt. 28:19–20; Luke 24:46–49).

From the Commentary

It was expected that rabbis would discuss theological matters in public, and the question the scribe (lawyer) asked in 10:25–37 was one that was often debated by the Jews. It was a good question asked with a bad motive, because the lawyer hoped to trap our Lord. However, Jesus trapped the lawyer!

Our Lord sent the man back to the law, not because the law saves us (Gal. 2:16, 21; 3:21), but because the law shows us that we need to be saved. There can be no real conversion without conviction, and the law is what God uses to convict sinners (Rom. 3:20).

The scribe gave the right answer, but he would not apply it personally to himself and admit his own lack of love for both God and his neighbor. So, instead of *being justified* by throwing himself on the mercy of God (Luke 18:9–14), he tried *to justify himself* and wriggle out of his predicament. He used the old debating tactic: "Define your terms! What do you mean by 'neighbor'? Who is my neighbor?"

—*Be Compassionate*, pages 135–36

9. How did Jesus use the law to turn the scribe's question back on himself? Why would a story that made the Samaritans look good and the Jews look bad be contentious for Jesus to tell? What reason might He have had for being deliberately contentious?

From the Commentary

Worship is at the heart of all that we are and all that we do in the Christian life. It is important that we be busy ambassadors, taking the message of the gospel to lost souls. It is also essential to be merciful Samaritans, seeking to help exploited and hurting people who need God's mercy. But before we can represent Christ as we should, or imitate Him in our caring ministry, we must spend time with Him and learn from Him. We must "take time to be holy."

Mary of Bethany is seen three times in the gospel record, and on each occasion, she is in the same place: at the feet of Jesus. She sat at His feet and listened to His Word (Luke 10:39), fell at His feet and shared her woe (John 11:32), and came to His feet and poured out her worship (John 12:3). It is interesting to note that in each of these instances, there is some kind of fragrance: in Luke 10, it is food; in John 11, it is death (John 11:39); and in John 12, it is perfume.

Mary and Martha are often contrasted as though each believer must make a choice: be a *worker* like Martha or a *worshipper* like Mary. Certainly our personalities and gifts are different, but that does not mean that the Christian life is an either/or situation.

—*Be Compassionate*, page 139

10. Read Luke 10:39; John 11:32; 12:3. What is consistent about Mary's approach to Jesus in each of these verses? What are the differences between Mary and Martha? How is it possible to follow Mary's example while still being active in the world?

Looking Inward

Take a moment to reflect on all that you've explored thus far in this study of Luke 9—10. Review your notes and answers and think about how each of these things matters in your life today.

Tips for Small Groups: To get the most out of this section, form pairs or trios and have group members take turns answering these questions. Be honest and as open as you can in this discussion, but most of all, be encouraging and supportive of others. Be sensitive to those who are going through particularly difficult times and don't press for people to speak if they're uncomfortable doing so.

11. Do you feel God has commissioned you to spread the good news? Why or why not? How do you do that? What helps you? What potentially gets in the way?

12. What are some of the things Jesus teaches that confuse you or trouble you? How do you deal with those things? What role does trust play when you're unsure what God is saying? What are some good ways to overcome your uncertainty?

13. Are you more naturally a Mary (worshipper) or a Martha (worker)? Explain. What can you do to become more balanced in how you live out your faith?

Going Forward

14. Think of one or two things that you have learned that you'd like to work on in the coming week. Remember that this is all about quality, not quantity. It's better to work on one specific area of life and do it well than to work on many and do poorly (or to be so overwhelmed that you simply don't try).

Do you want to learn how to balance worship and work? Be specific. Go back through Luke 9—10 and put a star next to the phrase or verse that is most encouraging to you. Consider memorizing this verse.

Real-Life Application Ideas: This week, practice both your Mary and Martha attributes in practical ways. Attend worship services and be intentional about personal worship times. Then also participate in worklike activities, whether volunteering at church or helping out at home or elsewhere. As you do this, focus on how each aspect of the Christian life can bring you closer to Christ.

Seeking Help

15. Write a prayer below (or simply pray one in silence), inviting God to work on your mind and heart in those areas you've noted in the Going Forward section. Be honest about your desires and fears.

Notes for Small Groups:

- *Look for ways to put into practice the things you wrote in the Going Forward section. Talk with other group members about your ideas and commit to being accountable to one another.*

- *During the coming week, ask the Holy Spirit to continue to reveal truth to you from what you've read and studied.*

- *Before you start the next lesson, read Luke 11. For more in-depth lesson preparation, read chapter 10, "Learning Life's Lessons," in* Be Compassionate.

Life Lessons
LUKE 11

Before you begin ...
- *Pray for the Holy Spirit to reveal truth and wisdom as you go through this lesson.*
- *Read Luke 11. This lesson references chapter 10 in* Be Compassionate. *It will be helpful for you to have your Bible and a copy of the commentary available as you work through this lesson.*

Getting Started

From the Commentary

We usually think of John the Baptist as a prophet and martyr, and yet our Lord's disciples remembered him as a man of prayer. John was a "miracle baby," filled with the Holy Spirit before he was born, and yet he had to pray. He was privileged to introduce the Messiah to Israel, and yet he had to pray. Jesus said that John was the greatest of the prophets (Luke 7:28), and yet John had to depend on prayer. If prayer was that vital to a man who had these many advantages, how much more important it ought to be to us who do not have these advantages!

John's disciples had to pray, and Jesus' disciples wanted to learn better how to pray.

—*Be Compassionate*, page 145

1. Why did the disciples ask Jesus to teach them to pray? What about prayer was difficult or confusing for them? How is that like the way believers today struggle with prayer? What does Jesus' answer teach us about prayer?

More to Consider: Read Luke 3:21; 5:16; 6:12; 9:18; and 9:28–29. What prompted each of these prayer opportunities? What do these verses tell us about Jesus' relationship with prayer?

2. Choose one verse or phrase from Luke 11 that stands out to you. This could be something you're intrigued by, something that makes you uncomfortable, something that puzzles you, something that resonates with you, or just something you want to examine further. Write that here.

Going Deeper

From the Commentary

> We call 11:2–4 "the Lord's Prayer," not because Jesus prayed it (He never had to ask for forgiveness), but because Jesus taught it. There is nothing wrong with praying this prayer personally or as part of a congregation, so long as we do it from a believing heart that is sincere and submitted. How easy it is to "recite" these words and not really mean them, but that can happen even when we sing and preach! The fault lies with us, not with this prayer.
>
> It has well been said that the purpose of prayer is not to get man's will done in heaven, but to get God's will done on earth. Prayer is not telling God what we want and then selfishly enjoying it. Prayer is asking God to use us to accomplish *what He wants* so that His name is glorified; His kingdom is extended and strengthened; and His will is done. I must test all of my personal requests by these overruling concerns if I expect God to hear and answer my prayers.
>
> —*Be Compassionate*, pages 146–47

3. In what ways is this prayer a "pattern prayer"? What does it teach us about our relationship with God? How does true prayer involve responsibilities? What are those responsibilities?

From the Commentary

> In 11:5–8, Jesus did not say that God is like this grouchy neighbor. In fact, He said just the opposite. If a tired and selfish neighbor finally meets the needs of a bothersome friend, how much more will a loving heavenly Father meet the needs of His own dear children! He is arguing from the lesser to the greater.
>
> God the Father is not like this neighbor, for He never sleeps, never gets impatient or irritable, is always generous, and delights in meeting the needs of His children. The friend at the door had to keep on knocking in order to get what he needed.
>
> —*Be Compassionate*, pages 147–48

4. How did Jesus use friendship to illustrate persistence in prayer? How is God unlike the friend at the door in the way He responds? Why is it so important to God that we learn persistence?

From Today's World

Prayer has been a part of most cultures since the dawn of time. In some cultures and religions, prayer is primarily ritualistic and structured; in others, it's more spontaneous. Some variation of prayer—supplication or conversation with a deity—is part of nearly every religion and even some nonreligious groups; the only difference is whom people pray to.

In America, you'll find prayer practiced outside of church in many public arenas, including sporting events (before, during, and after), at concerts (behind the scenes or on stage), at political events, and just about any other place where people gather in a group. It's in the movies, on TV, and at your favorite local restaurants. Prayer may be as much a part of our modern culture as it was in the early days of Christian faith.

5. How would you describe the role of public prayer in America today? How meaningful do you think it is? Why? What is its purpose? How is it different from private prayer?

From the Commentary

Why does our Father in heaven answer prayer? Not just to meet the needs of His children, but to meet them in such a way that it brings glory to His name. "Hallowed be thy name." *When God's people pray, God's reputation is at stake.* The way He takes care of His children is a witness to the world that He can be trusted. Phillips Brooks said that prayer is not overcoming God's reluctance; it is laying hold of His highest willingness. Persistence in prayer is not an attempt to change God's mind ("thy will be done") but to get ourselves to the place where He can trust us with the answer.

—*Be Compassionate,* page 148

6. Respond to this statement from above: Prayer is not overcoming God's reluctance; it is laying hold of His highest willingness. We're called to pray often and with sincerity. Why does the frequency of prayer matter to God? How does it prepare us to hear God?

From the Commentary

Luke 11:14–16 records the third miracle of deliverance our Lord performed that elicited from His enemies the accusation that He was in league with Satan (see Matt. 9:32–34; 12:22–37). Instead of rejoicing that God had sent a Redeemer, the religious leaders were rebelling against the truth of God's Word and seeking to discredit Christ's work and character. Imagine people being so blind that they could not distinguish a work of God from a work of Satan!

"Beelzebub" was one of the names of the Philistine god Baal (2 Kings 1:1–3); it means "lord of flies." A variant is "Beelzebul," which means "lord of the dwelling" and ties in with Christ's illustrations in Luke 11:18–26. The Jews often used this name when referring to Satan.

—*Be Compassionate*, page 149

7. Why did the people ask Jesus to prove He was working for God? Why wasn't the miracle enough? What kind of sign from heaven would have convinced them? Why was it dangerous to tempt God in this way?

From the Commentary

It is impossible to be neutral in this spiritual war (Luke 11:23; see also 9:50), for neutrality means standing against Him. There are two spiritual forces at work in the world, and we must choose between them. Satan is scattering and destroying, but Jesus Christ is gathering and building. We must make a choice, and if we choose to make *no* choice, we are really choosing against Him.

Jesus illustrated the danger of neutrality by telling the story of the man and the demon. The man's body was the demon's "house" (Luke 11:24; and note vv. 17 and 21). For some unknown reason, the demonic tenant decided to leave his "house" and go elsewhere. The man's condition improved immediately, *but the man did not invite God to come and dwell within*. In other words, the man remained neutral. What happened? The demon returned with seven other demons worse than himself, and the man's condition was abominable.

—*Be Compassionate*, page 150

8. Respond to this quote from Oswald Chambers in light of what Jesus said in the story about the man and the demon: "Neutrality in religion is always cowardice." Why is neutrality bad? Is it worse than disbelief or distrust? Explain.

From the Commentary

Because He knew what was in their hearts, Jesus was not impressed by the big crowds, but the disciples were. In order to keep the Twelve from being swayed by "success," Jesus gave them some insights into what was really happening as they ministered the Word. He used three illustrations to show the seriousness of spiritual opportunities.

(1) Jonah (vv. 29–30, 32). The leaders kept asking Jesus for a sign to prove that He was the Messiah. The only sign He promised was "the sign of Jonah the prophet," which is *death, burial, and resurrection.* It is the resurrection of our Lord that proves He is the Messiah, the Son of God (Rom. 1:4), and this is what Peter preached to Israel on the day of Pentecost (Acts 2:22ff.). The witness of the early church was centered on Christ's resurrection (Acts 1:22; 3:15; 5:30–32; 13:32–33). Jonah was a living miracle and so is our Lord Jesus Christ.

(2) Solomon (v. 31). The emphasis here is on the wisdom of a king, not the works of a prophet. The Queen of Sheba traveled many miles to hear the wisdom of Solomon (1 Kings 10), but here was the very Son of God *in their midst,* and the Jews would not believe His words! Even if Jesus had performed a sign, it would not have changed their hearts. They needed the living wisdom of God, but they were content with their stale religious tradition.

(3) Light (vv. 33–36). The third illustration was from daily life, not from history, and was one Jesus had used before (Matt. 6:22–23). God's Word is a light that shines in this dark world (Ps. 119:105; Prov. 6:23). But it is not enough that the light be shining *externally*, it must enter our lives before it can do any good. "The entrance of thy words giveth light; it giveth understanding unto the simple" (Ps. 119:130). The brightest sun cannot enable a blind man to see.

—Be Compassionate, pages 151–52

9. Review Luke 11:29–32. Why was it important at this moment for Jesus to emphasize the seriousness of the spiritual opportunity the people were facing? How might His hearers have felt being compared to Gentiles (the Ninevites and the Queen of Sheba)? Why would Luke be drawn to examples involving Gentiles?

More to Consider: Read John 8:12; 2 Cor. 4:3–6; Eph. 5:8–14. What do these verses tell us about being children of light? How do we maintain that light? How do we lose it? (See Luke 11:33.)

From the Commentary

Jesus gives us a "spiritual analysis" of the Pharisees in 11:37–54.

He exposed their folly (vv. 37–41). The basic error of the Pharisees was thinking that righteousness was only a matter of external actions, and they minimized internal attitudes. They were very careful to keep the outside clean, but they ignored the wickedness within. They seemed to forget that the same God who created the outside also created the inside, the "inner person" that also needs cleansing (Ps. 51:6, 10).

He denounced their sins (vv. 42–52). These six "woes" parallel the "woes" in Matthew 23. Jesus started with the sins of the Pharisees (Luke 11:42–44) and then turned to the sins of the scribes, for it was their interpretations of the law that formed the basis for the whole pharisaical system (Luke 11:45–52).

He aroused their anger (vv. 53–54). Hypocrites do not want their sins exposed; it hurts their reputation. Instead of opposing the Lord, these men should have been seeking His mercy. They deliberately began to attack Him with "catch questions" in hopes they could trap Him in some heresy and then arrest Him. What a disgraceful way to treat the Son of God!

—*Be Compassionate*, pages 153, 156

10. At this stage in Christ's ministry, why would a Pharisee invite Him to his home for a meal? Why didn't the Pharisee speak to Jesus in private about Jesus' decision not to practice the ceremonial washing before eating (Mark 7:2–4)? What was the point of not performing the ceremonial washing? How did Jesus take advantage of this opportunity to teach the Pharisee?

Looking Inward

Take a moment to reflect on all that you've explored thus far in this study of Luke 11. Review your notes and answers and think about how each of these things matters in your life today.

> *Tips for Small Groups: To get the most out of this section, form pairs or trios and have group members take turns answering these questions. Be honest and as open as you can in this discussion, but most of all, be encouraging and supportive of others. Be sensitive to those who are going through particularly difficult times and don't press for people to speak if they're uncomfortable doing so.*

11. Do you say the Lord's Prayer outside of group recitations? Why or why not? What does the Lord's Prayer do for you? How can it help you know how to pray?

12. Describe your prayer life. What does it look like on a daily basis? What priority do you give prayer at home? At work? With your family? What expectations do you have of prayer?

13. Have you ever tempted God to prove Himself with a miracle? Explain the circumstance. Why did you want God to perform a miracle? What was the result of your request? What did God teach you through that experience?

Going Forward

14. Think of one or two things that you have learned that you'd like to work on in the coming week. Remember that this is all about quality, not quantity. It's better to work on one specific area of life and do it well than to work on many and do poorly (or to be so overwhelmed that you simply don't try).

Do you want to develop a more regular prayer life? Be specific. Go back through Luke 11 and put a star next to the phrase or verse that is most encouraging to you. Consider memorizing this verse.

Real-Life Application Ideas: This week, start every day by reciting the Lord's Prayer (alone, or with your family members). Talk with family members or friends about each aspect of the Lord's Prayer and why each is an important part of your prayer life. Then compose an original prayer based on the pattern the Lord's Prayer gives you, and pray that at the end of each day. Ask God to help you learn more about what it really means to pray through this exercise.

Seeking Help

15. Write a prayer below (or simply pray one in silence), inviting God to work on your mind and heart in those areas you've noted in the Going Forward section. Be honest about your desires and fears.

Notes for Small Groups:

- *Look for ways to put into practice the things you wrote in the Going Forward section. Talk with other group members about your ideas and commit to being accountable to one another.*

- *During the coming week, ask the Holy Spirit to continue to reveal truth to you from what you've read and studied.*

- *Before you start the next lesson, read Luke 12—13. For more in-depth lesson preparation, read chapters 11, "Believer, Beware!," and 12, "Questions and Answers," in* Be Compassionate.

A Warning
LUKE 12—13

Before you begin …
- *Pray for the Holy Spirit to reveal truth and wisdom as you go through this lesson.*
- *Read Luke 12—13. This lesson references chapters 11 and 12 in* Be Compassionate. *It will be helpful for you to have your Bible and a copy of the commentary available as you work through this lesson.*

Getting Started

From the Commentary

The word *hypocrite* comes from a Greek word that means "an actor," "one who plays a part." There are hypocrites in every walk of life, people who try to impress others in order to hide their real selves. In the Christian life, a hypocrite is somebody who tries to appear more spiritual than he or she really is. These people know that they are pretending, and they hope they will not be found out. Their Christian life is only a shallow masquerade.

—*Be Compassionate*, pages 159–60

1. Review Luke 12:1–2. Why did Jesus give the warning against hypocrisy at this particular time? What temptations might the disciples have faced that could lead to hypocrisy? How can we keep hypocrisy out of our lives?

More to Consider: Read Matthew 6:1–18. How does doing things privately help us overcome hypocrisy? Does Jesus' instruction here mean that we should never pray in public? Explain.

2. Choose one verse or phrase from Luke 12—13 that stands out to you. This could be something you're intrigued by, something that makes you uncomfortable, something that puzzles you, something that resonates with you, or just something you want to examine further. Write that here.

Going Deeper

From the Commentary

The remedy for hypocrisy is to forget about what people may say and do and *fear God alone*. The fear of God is the fear that conquers all other fears, for the person who truly fears God need fear nothing else. All that men can do is kill the body, but God can condemn the soul! Since He is the final Judge, and He judges for eternity, it is logical that we put the fear of God ahead of everything else. Our God knows us and cares for us. He cares for the sparrows, and we are of more value than they, so what do we have to fear from men?

We must confess Christ openly (vv. 8–9). Once we have done this, we will have an easier time living the truth and avoiding hypocrisy. How can we fear men when we know Jesus Christ is confessing us before the Father in heaven? It is not important that men praise our names on earth, but it is important that God acknowledges us in heaven (see 2 Tim. 2:8–14).

We must depend on the Holy Spirit (vv. 10–12). Jesus appears to be contradicting Himself. In Luke 12:8–9, He demands that we openly confess Him, but in Luke 12:10, He says we can speak against Him and be forgiven. However, if we speak against the Spirit, there is no forgiveness! Does this mean that the Holy Spirit is more important than the Son of God?

—*Be Compassionate*, page 161

3. What does it look like to confess God openly (12:8–9)? How do we depend on the Holy Spirit when we do this (12:10–12)? How does fear sometimes prevent us from doing this? Why is fearing God so crucial in these situations?

From the Commentary

At this point, a man in the crowd interrupted Jesus and asked Him to solve a family problem. Rabbis were expected to help settle legal matters, but Jesus refused to get involved. Why? Because He knew that no answer He gave would solve the *real* problem, which was covetousness in the hearts of the two brothers. (The "you" in Luke 12:14 is plural.) As long as both men were greedy, *no* settlement would be satisfactory. Their greatest need was to have their hearts changed. Like too many people today, they wanted Jesus to serve them but not to save them.

Covetousness is an unquenchable thirst for getting more and more of something we think we need in order to be truly satisfied. It may be a thirst for money or the things that money can buy, or even a thirst for position and power. Jesus made it clear that true life does not depend on an abundance of possessions. He did not deny that we have certain basic needs (Matt. 6:32; 1 Tim. 6:17). He only affirmed that we will not make life richer by acquiring *more* of these things.

—*Be Compassionate*, pages 162–63

4. Review Luke 12:13–21. Mark Twain once defined *civilization* as "a limitless multiplication of unnecessary necessities." How does this relate to what Jesus is teaching in this passage? Can Christians be infected with covetousness and not know it? Explain. How does Paul's admonition in 1 Timothy 6:6–10 apply to all people, not just the rich and famous?

From the Commentary

The rich farmer in 12:22–34 worried because he had too much, but the disciples might be tempted to worry because they did not have enough! They had given up all they had in order to follow Christ. They were living by faith, and faith is always tested.

Worry is destructive. The word translated "anxious" in Luke 12:22 means "to be torn apart," and the phrase "doubtful mind" (Luke 12:29) means "to be held in suspense." It is the picture of a ship being tossed in a storm. Our English word *worry* comes from an old Anglo-Saxon word that means "to strangle." "Worry does not empty tomorrow of its sorrow," said Corrie ten Boom, "it empties today of its strength."

Worry is also deceptive. It gives us a false view of life, of itself, and of God. Worry convinces us that life is made up of what we eat and what we wear. We get so concerned about *the means* that we totally forget about *the end*, which is to glorify God (Matt. 6:33). There is a great difference between making a living and making a life.

Worry is deformative. It keeps us from growing, and it makes us like the unsaved in the world (Luke 12:30). In short, worry is unchristian; worry is a sin. How can we witness to a lost world and encourage them to put faith in Jesus Christ if we ourselves are doubting God and worrying? Is it not inconsistent to preach faith and yet not practice it? Late chaplain of the United States Senate Peter Marshall once prayed "that ulcers would not become the badge of our faith." Too often they are!

—*Be Compassionate*, pages 165–66

5. What were the early Christians tempted to worry about? Why is worry such a problem for believers today? What is Jesus' prescription for worry?

From the Commentary

Jesus shifted the emphasis from being worried about the present to being watchful about the future in 12:35–53. The themes in Luke 12 all go together, for one of the best ways to conquer hypocrisy, covetousness, and worry is to look for the Lord's return. When you are "living in the future tense," it is difficult for the things of the world to ensnare you. In this section, Jesus explained how we can be ready for His return.

Jewish weddings were held at night, and a bridegroom's servants would have to wait for their master to come home with his bride. The new husband would certainly not want to be kept waiting at the door with his bride! But the servants had to be sure they were ready to go to work, with their robes tucked under their girdles so they were free to move (see 1 Peter 1:13ff.).

To "watch" means to be alert, to be ready, not to be caught by surprise. That is the attitude we must have toward the second coming of Jesus Christ. His coming will be like that of a thief: unannounced and unexpected (Matt. 24:43; 1 Thess. 5:2; Rev. 16:15).

—*Be Compassionate*, page 167

6. Review Luke 12:35–40. What surprising things did the master in this story do? How are we in the same position the servants of the story were in? What does this story teach us about the importance of watching and waiting? What does watching and waiting look like in practice today?

From the Commentary

In Luke 12:54–59, we see two illustrations to impress on the crowds the importance of discernment and diligence in spiritual matters. First, He talked about the weather, and then He talked about a lawsuit.

(1) **Discernment (vv. 54–57).** If people were as discerning about spiritual things as they are about the weather, they would be better off! The crowd could predict a storm, but it could not foresee the coming judgment. It knew that the temperature was about to change, but it could not interpret the "signs of the times." The Jewish nation had the prophetic Scriptures for centuries and should have known what God was doing, but their religious leaders led them astray.

How tragic that men today can predict the movements of the heavenly bodies, split atoms, and even put men on the moon, but they are blind to what God is doing in the world. They know how to get to the stars, but they do not know how to get to heaven! Our educated world possesses a great deal of scientific knowledge but not much spiritual wisdom.

(2) **Diligence (vv. 58–59).** Anyone will do whatever is necessary to stay out of prison, but how many people will apply that same concern and diligence to stay out of hell? If lawyers and judges would examine God's Word as diligently as they examine their law books, they will gain a wisdom that the law cannot give.

—*Be Compassionate*, pages 169–70

7. What roles do discernment and diligence play in our faith lives? Why might Jesus have focused on these two themes at this point in His ministry? How might the disciples have been struggling with these issues? How do we struggle with them today?

From the Commentary

Pontius Pilate, the Roman governor, did not get along with the Jews because he was insensitive to their religious convictions. For example, he brought the official Roman ensigns into Jerusalem and infuriated the Jews who resented having Caesar's image in the Holy City. Pilate threatened to kill the protesters, *and they were willing to die*! Seeing their determination, the governor relented and moved the ensigns to Caesarea, but that did not stop the hostilities.

The atrocity mentioned in Luke 13:1 may have taken place when Pilate "appropriated" money from the temple treasury to help finance an aqueduct. A large crowd of angry Jews gathered in protest, so Pilate had soldiers *in civilian clothes* mingle with the mob. Using concealed weapons, the soldiers killed a number of innocent and unarmed Jews, and this only added to the Jews' hatred for their governor.

Since Jesus was going up to Jerusalem, anything He said about Pilate was sure to get there before Him. If He ignored the issue, the crowd would accuse Him of being pro-Roman and disloyal to His people. If He defended the Jews and accused Pilate, He would be in trouble with the Romans, and the Jewish leaders would have a good excuse to get Him arrested.

—*Be Compassionate*, pages 173–74

8. Review Luke 13:1–9. How did Jesus move the issue to a higher level and avoid politics? What did He deal with instead of Pilate's sins? How did Jesus make it clear that human tragedies are not always divine punishments? What's the message here for believers and how they judge others?

More to Consider: What application does the parable in Luke 13:6–9 have both for individuals and the nation of Israel? (See 2 Pet. 3:9 and Matt. 3:7–10.) How does the tree remind us of God's special goodness to Israel? (See Isa. 5:1–7; Rom. 9:1–5.) Why is it significant that the parable is open-ended?

From the Commentary

The events recorded in John 9—10 fit between Luke 13:21 and 22. Note in John 10:40–42 that Jesus then left Judea and went beyond the Jordan into Perea. The events of Luke 13:22—17:10 took place in Perea as the Lord gradually moved toward Jerusalem.

The scribes often discussed the question of how many people would be saved, and somebody asked Jesus to give His thoughts on the issue. As with the question about Pilate, Jesus immediately made the matter personal. "The question is not how many will be saved, but whether or not *you* will be saved! Get that settled first, and then we can discuss what you can do to help get others saved."

I sometimes receive "theological letters" from radio listeners who want to argue about predestination, election, and other difficult doctrines. When I reply, I usually ask them about their prayer life, their witnessing, and their work in the local church. That often ends the correspondence. Too many professed Christians want to discuss these profound doctrines, but they do not want to put them into practice by seeking to win people to Jesus Christ!

D. L. Moody prayed, "Lord, save the elect, and then elect some more!"

"Many … will seek to enter in, and shall not be able" (Luke 13:24). Why? The parable tells us why, and it focuses primarily on the Jewish people of that day. However, it has a personal application to all of us today.

Jesus pictured the kingdom as a great feast, with the patriarchs and prophets as honored guests (Luke 13:28). But many of the people who were invited waited too long to respond, and, when they arrived at the banquet hall, it was too late and the door was shut (see Matt. 22:1–14; Luke 14:15–24).

—*Be Compassionate*, pages 179–80

9. In the parable in Luke 13:23–30, why did the honored guests wait so long to respond to the invitation? (See Luke 9:23–26.) What role did pride play in their delay? What is the message of this parable for us today?

From the Commentary

Jesus was in Perea, which was ruled by Herod Antipas, son of Herod the Great. The Pharisees wanted to get Jesus back into Judea, where the religious leaders could watch Him and ultimately trap Him, so they tried to frighten Him away.

Herod had been perplexed by our Lord's ministry and was afraid that John the Baptist, whom he murdered, had come back from the dead (Luke 9:7–9). In fact, at one point, Herod wanted to meet Jesus so he could see Him perform a miracle (Luke 23:8)! But it appears that Herod's heart was getting harder, for now he threatened to kill Jesus. The warning the Pharisees gave (Luke 13:31) was undoubtedly true or Jesus would not have answered as He did.

Our Lord was not afraid of danger. He followed a "divine timetable" and nothing could harm Him. He was doing the will of God according to the Father's schedule (see John 2:4; 7:30; 8:20; 13:1; 17:1). It had been decreed from eternity that the Son of God would be crucified in Jerusalem at the Passover (1 Peter 1:20; Rev. 13:8), and even Herod Antipas could not hinder the purposes of God. Quite the contrary, our Lord's enemies only helped *fulfill* the will of God (Acts 2:23; 3:13–18).

Jesus used a bit of "holy sarcasm" in His reply. He compared Herod to a fox, an animal that was not held in high esteem by the Jews (Neh. 4:3). Known for its cunning,

144 \ The Wiersbe Bible Study Series: Luke 1—13

the fox was an apt illustration of the crafty Herod. Jesus had work to do, and He would accomplish it. After all, Jesus walked in the light (John 9:4; 11:9–10), and foxes went hunting in the darkness!

But Jesus also had a word to say about His nation: "It cannot be that a prophet perish out of Jerusalem" (Luke 13:33). This parallels what He had said to the scribes and Pharisees in Luke 11:47–51. The nation not only rejected God's loving invitation to His feast, but they even killed the servants who brought them the invitation!

—*Be Compassionate*, pages 181–82

10. Review Luke 13:31–35. Why would Herod have been worried that Jesus was John the Baptist come back to life? How might that have affected the way he responded to Jesus here and also later? What grieved Jesus about the people around Him? What did He say in His lament about the Jewish nation?

Looking Inward

Take a moment to reflect on all that you've explored thus far in this study of Luke 12—13. Review your notes and answers and think about how each of these things matters in your life today.

Tips for Small Groups: To get the most out of this section, form pairs or trios and have group members take turns answering these questions. Be honest and as open as you can in this discussion, but most of all, be encouraging and supportive of others. Be sensitive to those who are going through particularly difficult times and don't press for people to speak if they're uncomfortable doing so.

11. How do you deal with the hypocrisy of others? How do you avoid becoming a hypocrite yourself? Why is that important to you?

12. What are some ways you struggle with covetousness? Do you ever feel like you "deserve" things from God? Explain. How do you overcome the temptation to want more?

13. What does it mean to you to watch and wait for God's kingdom? Do you find it easy to wait? Why or why not? What are some ways you look forward to the coming kingdom? What are ways you can live in and enjoy the kingdom of God today?

Going Forward

14. Think of one or two things that you have learned that you'd like to work on in the coming week. Remember that this is all about quality, not quantity. It's better to work on one specific area of life and do it well than to work on many and do poorly (or to be so overwhelmed that you simply don't try).

Do you need to work on your tendency to be covetous? Be specific. Go back through Luke 12—13 and put a star next to the phrase or verse that is most encouraging to you. Consider memorizing this verse.

Real-Life Application Ideas: Jesus spoke out against covetousness in Luke 12. Take this week to do a personal inventory on all the "stuff" you have and all the things you wish you could have. This is a time to be honest about your desires—whether they're things you believe are necessary or things you simply want. Then talk with your spouse (if you're married) and a small-group leader or pastor about these desires, inviting their opinion on sorting through what is covetousness and what is reasonable, rational desire. The goal here isn't to give up your dreams or hopes but to identify the driving factor behind your wants. You may discover that you're doing a great job at pursuing your faith and caring for your family and aren't really struggling with coveting. Or you could find some areas where you might need to practice humility. Be open to however God speaks to you during this process.

Seeking Help

15. Write a prayer below (or simply pray one in silence), inviting God to work on your mind and heart in those areas you've noted in the Going Forward section. Be honest about your desires and fears.

Notes for Small Groups:

- *Look for ways to put into practice the things you wrote in the Going Forward section. Talk with other group members about your ideas and commit to being accountable to one another.*
- *During the coming week, ask the Holy Spirit to continue to reveal truth to you from what you've read and studied.*

Summary and Review

Notes for Small Groups: This session is a summary and review of this book. Because of that, it is shorter than the previous lessons. If you are using this in a small-group setting, consider combining this lesson with a time of fellowship or a shared meal.

Before you begin...
- *Pray for the Holy Spirit to reveal truth and wisdom as you go through this lesson.*
- *Briefly review the notes you made in the previous sessions. You will refer to previous sections throughout this bonus lesson.*

Looking Back

1. Over the past eight lessons, you've examined Luke 1—13. What expectations did you bring to this study? In what ways were those expectations met?

2. What is the most significant personal discovery you've made from this study?

3. What surprised you most about Luke 1—13? What, if anything, troubled you?

Progress Report

4. Take a few moments to review the Going Forward sections of the previous lessons. How would you rate your progress for each of the things you chose to work on? What adjustments, if any, do you need to make to continue on the path toward spiritual maturity?

5. In what ways have you grown closer to Christ during this study? Take a moment to celebrate those things. Then think of areas where you feel you still need to grow, and note those here. Make plans to revisit this study in a few weeks to review your growing faith.

Things to Pray About

6. Luke 1—13 is all about compassion. As you reflect on the ways in which Jesus expressed His compassion to followers and nonfollowers alike, consider how you might also show compassion in your daily walk.

7. The messages in Luke 1—13 include compassion for others, faith, prayer, the coming kingdom, and the power of God's love. Spend time praying about each of the topics you explored in this study.

8. Whether you've been studying this book in a small group or on your own, there are many other Christians working through the very same issues you discovered when examining Luke 1—13. Take time to pray for each of them, that God would reveal truth, that the Holy Spirit would guide you, and that each person might grow in spiritual maturity according to God's will.

A Blessing of Encouragement

Studying the Bible is one of the best ways to learn how to be more like Christ. Thanks for taking this step. In closing, let this blessing precede you and follow you into the next week while you continue to marinate in God's Word:

May God light your path to greater understanding as you review the truths found in Luke 1—13 and consider how they can help you grow closer to Christ.

THE WORLD STILL NEEDS HIS LOVE

Part of Dr. Warren W. Wiersbe's best-selling "BE" commentary series, *BE Compassionate* has now been updated with study questions and a new introduction by Ken Baugh. A respected pastor and Bible teacher, Dr. Wiersbe explores the compassionate life of Jesus. Filled with moving examples of Christ's ministry to people of all backgrounds, cultures, and beliefs, this study will inspire you to share His love with the world around you.